# TALKS ON TEACHING LITERATURE

# TALKS ON TEACHING LITERATURE

## ARLO BATES

MJP
PUBLISHERS

Chennai          New Delhi          Tirunelveli

**MJP PUBLISHERS**

**ISBN 978-93-87826-13-7**  **MJP Publishers**

All rights reserved
Printed and bound in India

No. 44, Nallathambi Street,
Triplicane, Chennai 600 005

MJP 444  © Publishers, 2018

**Publisher**  **C. Janarthanan**

**Project Editor**  **C. Ambica**

# Publisher's Note

The legacy of a country is in its varied cultural heritage, historical literature, developments in the field of economy and science. The top nations in the world are competing in the field of science, economy and literature. This vast legacy has to be conserved and documented so that it can be bestowed to the future generation. The knowledge of this legacy is slowly getting perished in the present generation due to lack of documentation.

Keeping this in mind, the concern with retrospective acquiring of rare books has been accented recently by the burgeoning reprint industry. MJP Publishers is gratified to retrieve the rare collections with a view to bring back those books that were landmarks in their time.

In this effort, a series of rare books would be republished under the banner, "MJP Publishers". The books in the reprint series have been carefully selected for their contemporary usefulness as well as their historical importance within the intellectual. We reconstruct the book with slight enhancements made for better presentation, without affecting the contents of the original edition.

Most of the works selected for republishing covers a huge range of subjects, from history to anthropology. We believe this reprint edition will be a service to the numerous researchers and practitioners active in this fascinating field. We allow readers to experience the wonder of peering into a scholarly work of the highest order and seminal significance.

**MJP PUBLISHERS**

# Contents


| I | The Problem | 1 |
|---|---|---|
| II | The Conditions | 8 |
| III | Some Difficulties | 20 |
| IV | Other Obstacles | 28 |
| V | Foundations of Work | 44 |
| VI | Preliminary Work | 54 |
| VII | The Inspirational Use of Literature | 64 |
| VIII | An Illustration | 70 |
| IX | Educational | 81 |
| X | Examinational | 89 |
| XI | The Study of Prose | 101 |
| XII | The Study of the Novel | 113 |
| XIII | The Study of "Macbeth" | 123 |
| XIV | Criticism | 145 |
| XV | Literary Workmanship | 155 |
| XVI | Literary Biography | 166 |
| XVII | Voluntary Reading | 170 |
| XVIII | In General | 178 |

# I

# The Problem

Few earnest teachers of literature have escaped those black moments when it seems perfectly evident that the one thing sure in connection with the whole business is that literature cannot be taught. If they are of sensitive conscience they are likely to have wondered at times whether it is honest to go on pretending to give instruction in a branch in which instruction was so obviously impossible. The more they consider, the more evident it is that if a pupil really learns anything *in* literature,—as distinguished from learning *about* literature,—he does it himself; and they cannot fail to see that as an art literature necessarily partakes of the nature of all art, the quality of being inexpressible and unexplainable in any language except its own.

The root of whatever difficulty exists in fulfilling the requirements of modern courses of training which have to do with literature is just this fact. Any art, as has been said often and often, exists simply and solely because it embodies and conveys what can be adequately expressed in no other form. A picture or a melody, a statue or a poem, gives delight and inspiration by qualities which could belong to nothing else. To teach painting or music or literature is at best to talk about these qualities. Words cannot express what the work or art expresses, or the work itself would be superfluous; and the teacher of literature is therefore apparently confronted with the task of endeavoring to impart what language itself cannot say.

So stated the proposition seems self-contradictory and absurd. Indeed it too often happens that in actual practice it is so. Teachers weary their very souls in necessarily fruitless endeavors to achieve the impossible, and fail in their work because they have not clearly apprehended what they could effect and what they should endeavor to effect. In any instruction it is of great importance to recognize natural and inevitable limitations, and nowhere is this more true than in any teaching which has to do with the fine arts. In other branches failure to perceive the natural restrictions of the subject limits the efficiency of the teacher; in the arts it not only utterly vitiates all work, but it gives students a fundamentally wrong conception of the very nature of that with which they are dealing.

In most studies the teacher has to do chiefly with the understanding, or, to put it more exactly, with the intellect of the pupil. In dealing with literature he must reckon constantly with the emotions also. If he cannot arouse the feelings and the imaginations of his students, he does not succeed in his work. Not only is this difficult in itself, but it calls for an emotional condition in the instructor which is not easily combined with the didactic mood required by teaching; a condition, moreover, which begets a sensitiveness to results much more keen than any disappointment likely to be excited by failure to carry a class triumphantly through a lesson in arithmetic or history. This sensitiveness constantly brings discouragement, and this in turn leads to renewed failure. In work which requires the happiest mood on the part of the teacher and the freest play of the imagination, the consciousness of any lack of success increases the difficulty a hundredfold. The teacher who is able by sheer force of determination to manage the stupidities of a dull algebra class, may fail signally in the attempt to make the same force carry him through an unappreciated exercise in "Macbeth." It is true that no teaching is effective unless the interest as well as the attention of the pupils is enlisted; but whereas in other branches this is a condition, in the case of literature it is a prime essential.

The teaching of literature, moreover, is less than useless if it is not educational as distinguished from examinational. It is greatly to be regretted that necessity compels the holding of examinations at all in a subject of which the worth is to be measured strictly by the extent to which it inspires the imagination and develops the character of the student. Any system of examinations is likely to be at best a makeshift made inevitable by existing conditions, and it is rendered tolerable only where teachers—often at the expense, under present school methods, of a stress of body and of soul to be appreciated only by those who have taught—are able to mingle a certain amount of education with the grinding drill of routine work. Examination papers hardly touch and can hardly show the results of literary training which are the only excuse for the presence of this branch in the school curriculum. Every faithful worker who is trying to do what is best for the children while fulfilling the requirements of the official powers above him is face to face with the fact that the tabulated returns of intermediates and finals do not in the least represent his best or most laboriously achieved success.

Under these conditions it is not strange that so many teachers are at a loss to know what they are expected to do or what they should attempt to do. If the teachers in the secondary schools of this country were brought together into some Palace of Truth where absolute honesty was forced upon them, it would be interesting and perhaps saddening to find how few could confidently assert that they have clear and logical ideas in regard to the teaching of literature. They would all be able to say that they dealt with certain specified books because such work is a prominent part of the school requirement; and many would, unless restrained by the truth-compelling power of their environment, add vague phrases about broadening the minds of the children. A pitiful number would be forced to confess that they had no clear conception of what they were to do beyond loading up the memories of the luckless young folk with certain dead information about books to be unloaded at the next examination, and there left forever. Too often "broadening the mind" of the young is simple flattening it out by the dead weight of lifeless and worthless fact.

This uncertainty in regard to what they are to do and how they are to do it is constantly evident in the complaints and inquiries of teachers. "How would you teach 'Macbeth'?" one asked me. "Do you think the sources of the plot should be thoroughly mastered?" Another wrote me that she had always tried to make the moral lesson of "Silas Marner" as clear and strong as possible, but that one of her boys had called her attention to the fact that no question on such a matter had ever appeared in the college entrance examination papers, and that she did not know what to do. A third said frankly that she could never see what there was in literature to teach, so she just took the questions suggested by a text-book and confined her attention to them. If these seem extreme cases, it is chiefly because they are put into words. Certainly the number of instructors who are virtually in the position of the third teacher is by no means small.

Even the editors of "school classics" are sometimes found to be no more enlightened than those they profess to aid, and not infrequently seem more anxious to have the appearance of doing a scholarly piece of work than one fitted for actual use. The devices they recommend for fixing the attention and enlightening the darkness of children in literary study are numerous; but not infrequently they are either ludicrous or pathetic. A striking example is that conspicuously futile method, the use of symbolic diagrams. The attempt to represent the poetry, the pathos, the passion of "The Merchant of Venice" or "Romeo and Juliet" by a diagram like a proposition in geometry seems to me not only the height of absurdity, but not a little profane. I have examined these cryptic combinations of lines, tangents, triangles, and circles, with more bewilderment than comprehension, I confess; generally with irritation; and always with the profound conviction that they could hardly be surpassed as a means of producing confusion worse confounded in the mind of any child whatever. Other schemes are only less wild, and while excellent and helpful text-books are not wanting, not a few show evidence that the writers were as little sure of what they were trying to effect, or of how it were best effected, as the most bewildered teacher who might unadvisedly come to them for enlightenment.

Instruction in literature as it exists to-day in the common schools of this country is almost always painstaking and conscientious; but it is by no means always intelligent. The teachers who resort to diagrams are sincerely in earnest, and no less faithful are those who at the expense of most exhausting labor are dragging classes through the morass of questions suggested by the least desirable of school editions of college requirements. They dose their pupils with notes as Mrs. Squeers dosed the poor wretches at Dotheboys Hall with brimstone and treacle. The result is much the same in both cases.

> "Oh! Nonsense," rejoined Mrs. Squeers. . . . "They have brimstone and treacle, partly because if they hadn't something or other in the way of medicine they'd be always . . . giving a world of trouble, and partly because it spoils their appetites, and comes cheaper than breakfast and dinner."

Certainly any child, no matter how great his natural appetite for literature, must find the desire greatly diminished after a dose of text-book notes.

The difficulties of teachers in handling this branch of instruction have been increased by the system under which work must be carried on. The tremendous problem of educating children in masses has yet to be solved, and it is at least doubtful if it can be worked out successfully without a very substantial diminution of the requirements now insisted upon. Certainly it is hardly conceivable that with the curriculum as crowded as it is at present any teacher could do much in the common schools with the teaching of literature. The pedagogic committees who have fixed the college entrance requirements, moreover, seem to have acted largely along conventional lines. In the third place the spirit of the time is out of sympathy with art, and the variety and insistence of outside calls on the attention and interest of the children make demands so great as to leave the mind dull to finer impressions. To the boy eager over football, the circus, and the automobile race he is to see when school is out, even an inspired teacher may talk in vain about Dr. Primrose, Lady Macbeth, or any other of the immortals. Ears accustomed to the strident measures of the modern street-song are not easily beguiled by the music of Milton, and yet the teacher of to-day is expected to persuade his flock that they should prefer "L'Allegro" to the vulgar but rollicking "rag-time" comic songs of dime-museum and alley. Under circumstances so adverse, it is not to be wondered at that teachers are not only discouraged but often bewildered.

What happens in many cases is sufficiently well shown by this extract from a freshman composition, in which the writer frankly gives an account of his training in English literature in a high school not twenty-five miles from Boston:

> Very special attention was paid to the instruction of the classics as to what the examinations require. As closely as possible the faculty determine the scope of the examinations, and the class is drilled in that work especially. Examination papers are procured for several years back, and are given to the students as regular high school examinations, and as samples of the kind of questions to be expected. The instructors notice especial questions that are often repeated in examination papers, warn the pupils of them, and even go so far as to estimate when the question will be used again. I have heard in the classroom, "This question was given three years ago, and it is about due again. They ask it every three or four years."

Another boy wrote, in the same set of themes, that he had taken the examination in the autumn, and added:

On the June examinations I noticed that there was nothing about Milton, so I studied Milton with heart and soul.

Here we find stated plainly what everybody connected with teaching knows to be common, and indeed what under the present system is almost inevitable. I know of many schools of no inconsiderable standing where in all branches old examination papers, if not used as the text-books, are at least the actual guide to all work done in the last year of fitting for college. This is perhaps only human, and it is easy to understand; but it certainly is not education, and of that fact both students and teachers are entirely well aware. All this I say with no intention of blaming anybody for what is the result of difficult conditions. It is not well, however, to ignore what is perfectly well known, and what is one of the important difficulties of the situation.

The problem, then, which confronts the teacher in the secondary school is twofold. He has to decide in the first place what the teaching of literature can and should legitimately accomplish, and in the second, by what means this may most surely and effectively be done. In a word, although work in this line has been going on multitudinously and confusedly for years, we are yet far from sufficiently definite ideas why and how literature should be taught to children.

II

# The Conditions

The inclusion of literature in the list of common school studies, however the original intent may have been lost sight of, was undoubtedly made in the interest of general culture. It is not certain that those who put it in had definite conceptions of methods or results, but unquestionably their idea was to aid the development of the children's minds by helping them to appreciate and to assimilate thoughts of nobility and of beauty, and by fostering a love for literature which should lead them to go on acquiring these from the masterpieces. How clear and well defined in the minds of educators this idea was it is needless to inquire. It is enough that it was undoubtedly sincere, and that it was founded on a genuine faith in the broadening and elevating influence of art.

The importance of literature as a means of mental development used to be taken for granted. Our fathers and grandfathers had for the classics a reverence which the rising generation looks back to as a phase of antiquated superstition, hardly more reasonable than the worship of sacred wells or a belief in goblins. So much stress is now laid upon the tangible and the material as the only genuine values, that everything less obvious is discredited. The tendency is to take only direct results into consideration; and influences which serve rather to elevate character than to aid in money-getting are at best looked upon with toleration.

That sense of mankind, however, which depends upon the perception of the few, and which in the long run forms the opinion of society in spite of everything, holds still to the importance of literature in any intelligent scheme of education. The popular disbelief makes enormously difficult the work of the teacher, but the force of the conviction of the wise minority keeps this branch in the schools. The sincere teacher, therefore, naturally tries to analyze effects, and to discern possibilities, in order to discover upon what facts the belief in the educational value of the study of literature properly rests.

The most obvious reasons for the study of literature may be quickly disposed of. It is well for a student to be reasonably familiar with the history of literature, with the names and periods of great writers. This adds to his chances of appearing to advantage in the world, and especially in that portion of society where he can least afford to be at a disadvantage. He is provided with facts about books and authors quite as much to protect him from the ill effects of appearing ignorant as for any direct influence this knowledge will have on his mind. Whatever the tendency of the times to undervalue in daily life acquaintance with the more refined side of human knowledge, the fact remains that to betray ignorance in these lines may bring real harm to a person's social standing. Every one recognizes that among educated people a lad is better able to make his way if he does not confound the age of Shakespeare with that of Browning, and if he is able to distinguish between Edmund Spenser and Herbert Spencer. Such information may not be specially vital, but it is worth possessing.

Considerations of this sort, however, are evidently not of weight enough to account for the place of the study in the schools, and still less to excuse the amount of time and attention bestowed upon it. The same line of reasoning would defend the introduction of dancing, because

> Those move easiest who have learned to dance.

More important and more far-reaching reasons must be found to satisfy the teacher, and to hearten him for the severe labor of working with class after class in the effort, not always successful, of arousing interest and enthusiasm over the writings which go by the name of English Classics. Some of these I may specify briefly. To deal with them exhaustively would take a book in itself, and would leave no room for the consideration of methods.

A careful and intelligent study of masterpieces of prose or verse, the teacher soon perceives, must develop greatly the student's sense of the value of words. This is not the highest function of this work, but it is by no means one to be despised. Literary study affords opportunities for training of this sort which are not to be found elsewhere; and a sensitiveness to word-values is with a child the beginning of wisdom.

Children too often acquire and adults follow the habit of accepting words instead of ideas. A genuine appreciation of the worth of language is after all the chief outward sign of the distinction between the wise man and the dullard. One is content to receive speech as sterling coin, and the other perceives that words are but counters. If students could but appreciate the difference between apprehending and comprehending what they are taught, between learning words and assimilating ideas, the intellectual millennium would be at hand. Children need to learn that the sentence is after all only the envelope, only the vehicle for the thought. Everybody agrees to this theoretically, but practically the fact is generally ignored. The child is father to the man in nothing else more surely than in the trait of accepting in perfect good faith empty words as complete and satisfactory in themselves. The habit of being content with phrases once bred into a child can be eradicated by nothing short of severe intellectual surgery.

To say that words are received as sufficient in themselves and not as conveying ideas sounds like a paradox; but there are few of us who may not at once make a personal application and find an illustration in the common phrases and formulas of our life. Perhaps none of us are free from the fault of sometimes substituting empty phrases for vital rules of conduct. The most simple and the most tremendous facts of human life are often known only as lifeless statements rather than realized as vibrant truths. With children the language of text-book or classroom is so likely to be repeated by rote and remembered mechanically that constant vigilance on the part of the teacher can hardly overcome the evil. Force the boy who on the college entrance examination paper writes fluently that "Milton is the poet of sublimity" to try to define, even to himself, what the statement means, and the result is confusion. He meant nothing. He had the words, but they had never conveyed to him a thought. Language should be the servant of the mind, but never was servant that so constantly and so successfully usurped the place of master.

Children must be taught, and taught not simply by precept but by experience, to realize that the value of the word lies solely in its efficiency as a vehicle of thought. They must learn to appreciate as well as to know mechanically that language is to be estimated by its effect in communicating the idea, and that to be satisfied with words for themselves is obvious folly. For enforcing this fact literature is especially valuable. It is hardly possible in even the most superficial work on a play of Shakespeare, for instance, for the reader to fail to perceive how the idea burns through the word, how wide is the difference between the mere apprehension of the language and the comprehension of the poet's meaning. In the study of great poetry the impossibility of resting satisfied with anything short of the ideas is so strongly brought out that it cannot be ignored or forgotten; and in this way pupils are impressed with the value of words.

This sensitiveness to the value of words in general is closely coupled with an appreciation of the force of words in particular, of what may be called word-values. The power of appreciating that a word is merely a messenger bringing an idea, is naturally connected with the ability to distinguish with exactness the nature and the value of the thought which the messenger presents. To feel the need of knowing clearly and surely the thought expressed inevitably leads to precision and delicacy in distinguishing the significance and force of language. When once a child appreciates the difference between the accepting of what he reads vaguely or mechanically and the getting from it its full meaning, he is eager to have it all; he finds delight in the intellectual exercise of searching out each hidden suggestion and in the sense of possession which belongs to achieving the thought of the master. It is not to be expected that our pupils shall be able to receive in its full richness the deepest thought of the poets, but they none the less find delight in possessing it to the extent of their abilities. The point is too obvious to need expansion; but every instructor will recognize its great importance.

Obvious as is this importance of the sense of the value of words and a sensitiveness to word-values, it is not infrequently overlooked. Teachers see the need of a knowledge of the meaning of terms and phrases in a particular selection without stopping to think of the prime value of the principle involved, or indeed that a general principle is involved at all. Still more often they fail to perceive all that logically follows. In exact, vital realization of the full force of language lies the secret of sharing the wisdom of the ages. If students can be trained to penetrate through the word of the printed page to the thought, they are brought into communication with the master-minds of the race. It is not learning to read in the common, primary acceptation of the term that opens for the young the thought of the race; but learning to read in the higher and deeper sense of receiving the word only as a symbol behind and beyond which the thought lies concealed from the ordinary and superficial reader.

Most of all is it the business of the young to learn about life. Whatever does not tend, directly or indirectly, to make the child better acquainted with the world he has come into, with how he must and how he should bear himself under its complex conditions, is of small value as far as education goes. Of rules for conduct he is given plenty as to matters of morality and of religion. Moral laws and religious precepts are good, and could they accomplish all that is sometimes expected of them, life would quickly be a different matter, and teachers would find themselves living in an earthly paradise. Unhappily these excellent maxims effect in actual life far less than is to be desired. Not infrequently the urchin who has been stuffed with moral admonitions as a doll with sawdust shows in his conduct no regard for them other than a fine zeal in scorning them. Children are seldom much affected by explicit directions in regard to conduct. They must be reached by indirection, and they are moulded less by what they recognize as intentionally wise views of life than by those which they receive unconsciously. The more just these unrecognized ideas of themselves and of the world are, the greater is the chance that they will develop a character well balanced and well adjusted to the conditions of human life.

Children live in a world largely made up of half-perceptions, of misunderstandings, and of dreams; a world pathetically full of guesses. They must depend largely upon appearances, and constantly confound what seems with what really is. They learn but slowly, however, to shape their beliefs or their emotions by conventionality. They do not easily acquire the vice of accepting shams because some authority has endorsed these. All of us are likely to have had queerly uncomfortable moments when we have found ourselves confounded and reproved by the unflinching honesty of the child; and we have been forced to confess, at least to ourselves, that much of our admiration is mere affectation, many of our professions unadulterated truckling to some authority in which after all we have little real faith. Children are naturally too unsophisticated for self-deception of this sort. They confound substance and shadow, but they do it in good faith and with no affectations. They are therefore at the place where they most need sound and sure help to apprehend and to comprehend those things which their elders call the realities of life.

What human nature and human life are like is learned most quickly and most surely from the best literature. The outward, the evident conditions of society and of humanity may perhaps be best obtained by children from the events of every-day existence; but in all that goes deeper the wisdom of great writers is the surest guide.

On the face of it such a proposition may not seem self-evident, and to not a few teachers it is likely to appear a little absurd. Children, it is evident, learn the realities of life by living. They perceive physical truth by the persuasive force of actual experience: by tumbling down and bumping their precious noses; by unmistakably impressive contact with the fist of a pugnacious school-fellow; by being hungry or uncomfortably stuffed with Thanksgiving turkey; by heat and by cold, by sweets or by sours, by hardness or by softness. Certainly through such means as these the child gains knowledge and develops mentally; but the process is inevitably slow. Most of all is the growth in the youthful mind of general deductions and the perception of underlying principles extremely gradual. He does not learn quickly enough that certain lines of conduct are likely to lead to unfortunate ends. Even when this is grasped, he has not come to appreciate what human laws underlie the whole matter; nor is he in the least likely to realize them so fully as to shape by them his conduct in the steadily more and more complicated affairs of life.

The small boy learns the wisdom of moderation from the stomach-ache which follows too much plum-pudding or too many green apples—if the pain is often enough repeated. The matter, however, is apt to present itself to his mind as a sort of tacit bargain between himself and Fate: so many green apples, so much stomach-ache; so much self-indulgence and so much pain, and the account is balanced. Life is not so simple as this; and that Fate does not make bargains so direct is learned from experience so gradually as often to be learned too late. To tell this to a child is of very little effect; for even if he believes it with his childish intelligence, he can hardly feel the intimate links which bind all humanity together, and make him subject to the same conditions that rule his elders and instructors.

The phrase "realities of life," moreover, includes not only sensible—that is, material—facts and conditions, but the more subtle things of inner existence. A hundred persons are able to gather facts, while very few are capable of drawing from them adequate conclusions or of perceiving how one truth bears upon another. A very moderate degree of intelligence is required for analysis as compared to that necessary for synthesis. The power "to put two and two together," as the common phrase has it, grows slowly in the mind of a child. Within a limited range children appreciate that one fact is somehow joined to another; and indeed the education which life gives consists chiefly in expanding this perception. The connection between touching a hot coal and being burned brings home the plain physical relations early. The connection between disobedience and unpleasant consequences will be borne in upon the youthful consciousness according to the sharpness of discipline by which it is enforced; and so on to the end of the chapter. To perceive a relation and to appreciate what that relation is are, however, different matters. The understanding of the nature of breaking rules and suffering in consequence involves a perception of underlying principle, and some comprehension of the real nature of these principles.

The part which literature may play in giving children, and for that matter their elders, a vivid perception of moral laws is shown by the use which has been made of fables and moral tales. The parables of Scripture illustrate the point. Of the habit of making literature directly a vehicle for moral instruction by the drawing of morals I shall have something to say later; but the extent to which this has been done at least serves here to make clearer what we mean by saying that in this study the child learns general principles and their relation. The small child, for instance, who is told in tender years that ingeniously virtuous fable which relates the heroic doings of little George Washington and his immortal hatchet, gets some idea of a connection between virtue and joy in the abstract. A notion faint, but none the less genuine, remains in his mind that some real connection exists between truth and desirability; and the same sort of thing holds true in cases where the teaching is less directly didactic.

The directly didactic is likely to be most in evidence in the training of children, and so affords convenient illustration of the illuminating effect of literature on young minds. Despite the fact that I disbelieve in reading into any tale or poem a moral which is not expressly put there by the author, and that I hold more strongly yet to the belief that the most marked and most lasting effects of imaginative work are indirect, I am not without a perception of the value at a certain stage of human development of the direct moral of the fable and the improving tale. A small lad of ten within the range of my observation, upon whom had been lavished an abundance, and perhaps even a superabundance, of moral precept, astonished and disconcerted his mother by remarking with delightful naïveté that he had at school been reading "The Little Merchant," in Miss Edgeworth's "Parents' Assistant," and that from it he had learned how mean and foolish it is to lie. "But, my dear boy," the mother cried in dismay, "I've been telling you that ever since you were born!" "Oh, well," responded the lad, with the unconsciously brutal frankness of his years, "but that never interested me." The obvious moral teaching that had made no impression when offered as a bare precept had been effective to him when presented as an appeal to his feeling.

Through imaginative literature abstract truths are made to have for the child a reality which is given to them by the experiences of daily life only by the slowest of degrees. Children rarely generalize, except in matters of personal feeling and in the regions of general misapprehension. A child easily receives the fact of the moment for a truth of all time: if he is miserable, for instance, he is very apt to feel that he must always be in that doleful condition; but this is in no real sense a generalization. It is more than half self-deception. Any child, however, who has been thrilled by a single line of imaginative poetry has—even if unconsciously—come into direct touch with a wide and humanly universal truth.

Especially and essentially is this to be said of truth which has to do with human feeling, the universal truth of the emotions. The man or the woman into whom the school-boy or girl is to grow will in shaping life be guided chiefly by the feelings. Whether the ordinary mortal lives well or ill, basely or nobly, dully or vividly, is practically determined by what he feels. However much the convictions have to do in ordering conduct, feeling has more, and conviction itself is with most mortals inseparably bound up with the emotions. The highest office of education is to develop the emotions highly and nobly; and it is no less essential to the intellectual than to the moral well-being of the child that he be bred to feel as deeply and as wholesomely as possible. Every teacher knows that in dealing with children the ultimate appeal is to their feelings. If a crisis arises in school-life it is to the emotions that the matter is inevitably referred, whether the instructor likes this or not, and whether the appeal is made openly or is indirect and tacit. Teaching must deal with the sentiments as well as with the understanding. That no other means of training and properly developing the feelings of youth is so efficient as literature seems to me a proposition too self-evident to need further comment.

Enthusiasm is so closely connected with the cultivation and training of the emotions that it is not easy to draw a line between them. While there is certainly no need to enlarge here upon the worth of enthusiasm in education or in life, or upon literature as a means of arousing it, it is worth while to emphasize the extent to which the mind of youth may be affected by enthusiasm. The effects are naturally often so indirect or intangible as not to be easily measured, but often, too, they are direct and practical. Some years ago in a country school in eastern Maine was still paramount the old-time Greenleaf's "Arithmetic" which we elders remember with mixed feelings. The law of education in those days, when children were still expected to do things which were mapped out for them and to follow a course of study whether it chanced to please their individual fancy or not, enforced the mastering of everything in the text-book, even to sundry weird processes with queer names such as "Alligation Alternate" and the like. The teacher of this particular school, a plucky morsel of New England womanhood, not much bigger than a chickadee, set herself resolutely to carry through the arithmetic a class of farmer lads, better at the plow than in mathematics. What happened she told me twenty-five years ago, and I am still able to call up the vision of the air half of defiance, half of amusement with which she said: "The boys were in a perfectly hopeless muddle. I had explained and explained, until I wished I could either cry like a woman or be a man and swear! The third day I had an inspiration. In the very middle of the recitation, I told them to shut up their books, and I cleaned every mark of the lesson off of the blackboard. Then without a word of explanation I began to tell them a little about the pamphlet Sir Walter Raleigh wrote about the 'Revenge;' and then I began to recite Tennyson's ballad—which was new then. I was wrought up to the very top-notch anyway, and I just gave that ballad for all there was in me. They were dazed a minute, and then they pricked up their ears, their eyes began to shine, and I had them. We kindled each other, and by the time I got through the tears were running down my cheeks for simple excitement. When I got to the end, you could just feel the hush. Then I told them to go outdoors and snow-ball for ten minutes, and then to come in and conquer that lesson. They were great, rough farmer boys, you understand; but the moment they were outside, they gave a cheer, just to express things they couldn't have put into words. When they came in they were alive to the ends of their fingers, and we went over that old Alligation with a perfect rush." This sort of thing would not be possible anywhere outside of the old-fashioned country school, but it is a capital illustration of the way in which poetry may stir the enthusiasm.

More valuable still, because at once deeper and most lasting, is the effect of literature in nourishing imagination. The real progress which children make in education—the assimilation of the knowledge which they receive—depends largely upon this power. In many branches of study this is easily evident. What a child actually knows of geography or of history obviously depends upon the extent to which his mind is able to make real places or events remote in space or in time. The same is true of those studies where the fact is not so evident; and it is hardly too much to say that the advance of any student in higher education is measured by the development of his imagination.

The teacher of literature in the secondary schools, then, is to consider that although his work is primarily done as a part of the school requirement, he need not be without some clear and deliberate intention in regard to the permanent effect upon the education and so upon the character of the pupil. He may treat the getting of his charges through the examinations as a purely secondary matter; a matter, moreover, which is practically sure to be accomplished if the greater and better purposes of the study have been secured. Besides a general knowledge of literary history, the student should gain from his training in the secondary school a vivid sense of the importance and value of words; an appreciation of word-values as shown in actual use by the masters; should increase in knowledge of life, and as it were gain experience vicariously, so as to advance in perception of intellectual and moral values; should be advanced in the control of the feelings; in enthusiasm; and in the development of that noblest of faculties, the imagination.

# III

# Some Difficulties

To deal clearly with the work of teaching, it is first of all essential to deal frankly. In order that suggestions in regard to instruction in literature may be of practical value, we must be entirely honest in admitting and in facing whatever difficulties lie in the way and whatever limitations are imposed by the conditions under which the work is done.

As things are at present arranged, an instructor, it seems not unjust to say, must decide how far he is able to mingle genuine education with the routine work which the system imposes upon him. If he has not the power to settle this question, or if he is lacking in the disposition to propose the question to himself, his labor is inevitably confined chiefly to routine. His students are turned out examination-perfect, it may be, but with minds as fatally cramped and checked as the feet of a Chinese lady. If literature has a high and important function in education, the teacher must consider deeply both what that function is and how he is best to develop it.

The failure on the part of instructors to do this makes much of the work done in the secondary grades so mechanical as to be of the smallest possible use so far as the expansion of the mind and of the character of children is concerned. For a pupil in the lower grades the first purpose of any and of all school-work should be to teach him to use his mind,—to think. The actual acquirement of facts is of importance really slight as compared to the value of this. If at twelve he knows how to read and to write, is sound on the multiplication-table, is familiar with the outlines of grammar and the broadest divisions of geography, yet is accustomed to think for himself in regard to the facts which he perceives from life or receives from books, he may be regarded as admirably well on in the education which he is to gain from the schools. Indeed, if he have learned to think, he is excellently started even if he have accomplished nothing further than simply to read and to write.

In these years of child-life the study of literature can legitimately have but two objects: it may and should minister to the delight of youth, that so the taste for good books be fostered and as it were inbred; and it should nourish the power of thinking. Whatever is beyond this has no place in the lower grades, and personally I am entirely free to say that much that is now called "the study of literature" is the sort of elaborate work which belongs in the college or nowhere. Few students are qualified to "study"—as the term is commonly interpreted—literature until they are advanced further than the boys and girls admitted to our high schools; further, indeed, than many who are allowed to enter the universities. The great majority of those who grind laboriously through the college entrance requirements in English are utterly unequal to the work and get from it little of value and a good deal of harm.

What should be done in the lower grades, and usually all that can with profit be attempted in the secondary schools anywhere, is to cultivate in the children a love of literature and some appreciation of it: appreciation intelligent, I mean, but not analytic. I would have the secondary schools do little with the history of authors, less with the criticism of style, and have no more explanation of difficulties of language and of structure than is necessary for the student's enjoyment. In a time when the draughts made by daily life upon the attention of the young are so tremendous, when the pressure of the more immediately practical branches of instruction is so great, to add drudgery in connection with literature seems to me completely futile and doubly wrong. The supreme test of success in whatever work in literature is done in schools of the secondary grades should be, according to my conviction, whether it has given delight, has fostered a love of whatever is best in imaginative writings and in life.

The natural abilities of children differ widely, and perhaps more difference still is made by the home influences in which they pass their earliest years. What should be done in the nursery can never be fully made up in the school, and what should be breathed in from an atmosphere of cultivation can never be imparted by instruction. It is manifestly impossible to interest all in the artistic side of life to the same extent, just as it is idle to hope to teach all to draw with equal skill. This does not alter the direction of effort. The teacher must recognize and accept natural limitations, but not on that account be satisfied with aiming at less admirable results.

Whatever are the conditions, it is possible to do something to foster a love of what is really good in literature, and to avoid the substitution of formal drill in the history of authors, the study of conundrums concerning the sources of plots, the meaning of obsolete words, and like pedantic pedagogics, for the friendly and vital study of what should be a warm, live topic. If young folk can be made really to care for good books, not only is substantial and lasting good gained, but most that is now attempted is more surely secured. William Blake declares that the truth can never be told so as to be understood and not be believed. In the same way it may be said that if children can be trained to recognize the characteristics of good literature, they are sure, in nine cases out of ten at least, to care for it.

This is the work which properly belongs to the secondary schools; and it is quite as much as they can be expected to do even up to the close of the high school course. I am personally unable to see what good is accomplished by taking any body of school-children that ever came under my own observation,—and the question must be judged by personal experience,—and drilling them in such matters as the following. I have taken these notes almost at random from approved school editions of the classics, and they seem to me to be fairly representative.

> Some striking resemblances in the incantation scenes in "Macbeth" and Middleton's "Witch" have led to a somewhat generally accepted belief that Thomas Middleton was answerable for the alleged un-Shakespearean portions of "Macbeth."

> Shakespeare's indebtedness in "Midsummer's Night's Dream" to "Il Percone" admits of no dispute.

> The incident of a Jew whetting his knife like Shylock occurs in a Latin play, "Machiavellus," performed at St. John's College, Cambridge, at Christmas, 1597.

The opening note in a popular edition of "Silas Marner" is a comment upon this passage:

> The questionable sound of Silas's loom, so unlike the natural, cheerful trotting of the winnowing-machine, or the simple rhythm of the flail, had a half-fearful fascination for the Raveloe boys.

The note reads as follows:

> The hand-loom, once found in every village and hamlet, was controlled by the action of the feet on the treadles, and worked by the hands. A figure representing the parts may be found in "Johnson's Cyclopædia." The longer article on "Weaving" in the "Encyclopædia Britannica" may also be consulted. The rattle of the loom was in direct contrast to the "cheerful trotting" of the winnowing-machine— an old-fashioned hand-machine for separating the chaff from the grain by means of wind produced by revolving fans. The flail, still in common use for threshing grain by hand, consists of a wooden staff or handle, hung on a club called a swiple, so as to turn easily.

If the end of the study of fiction is the acquirement of dry facts, this note may pass. I have purposely selected an example which is not worse than the average, and which may perhaps be supposed to have an excuse in the consideration that so many readers may be ignorant of all the contrivances mentioned; but can any person with a sense of humor suppose that a real boy is to get any proper enjoyment out of a story when he is at the outset asked to consult a couple of cyclopædias, and is interrupted in his reading by comments of this sort? The real point of the passage, moreover,—the literary significance,—the fact that the boys of Raveloe heard the winnowing-machine and threshing-flail daily, and so were attracted by the novelty of Marner's weaving, with the use of this by George Eliot to emphasize the weaver's isolation in the neighborhood, is left utterly unnoticed.

Were it worth while, I could give from text-books in general use examples more unsatisfactory than these; but this is a fair sample of the things which are administered to pupils in the name of literary study. The students are not interested in these details; and I am inclined to believe that most of the teachers who mistakenly feel obliged to drill classes in them could not honestly say that they themselves care a fig for such barren facts. It is no wonder that out of the school course young folk so often get the notion that literature is dull. In a recent entrance paper a boy wrote as follows:

> I could never understand why so much time has to be given in school to old books just because they have been known a long time. It would be better if we could have given the time to something useful.

He said what many boys feel, and what not a few of them have thought out frankly to themselves, although perhaps few would express it so squarely. If the study of literature means no more than is represented by work on notes and the history of books and authors, I most fully agree with him.

Some of the books at present included in the college entrance requirement, it must be added, lend themselves too much to unintelligent pedantry. Undoubtedly much thought has been given to the selection, although perhaps less sympathetic consideration of child nature. The result is not in all cases satisfactory. To foster a taste for poetry a teacher may, it is true, do much with "Julius Cæsar," but I have yet to see the class of undergraduates with which I should personally hope to arouse enthusiasm with "L'Allegro," "Il Penseroso," "Lycidas," or "Comus." I may be simply confessing my own limitations, but I should think all of these poems, magnificent in themselves, hardly fitted for the boys and girls who are found in our public schools. I have extracted from more than one teacher a confession of entire inability to take pleasure in the Milton which they assure their pupils is beautiful; and while this is an arraignment of instructors rather than of the works, it is significant of the attitude the honest minds of children are likely to take.

By way of making things worse, scholars are drilled in Macaulay's "Milton."[1] The inclusion of this essay, the product of the author's 'prentice hand, is most lamentable. The philistinism of Macaulay is here rampant; and the one thing which students are sure to get from the essay is the conception that poetry is the product of barbarism, to be outgrown and cast aside when civilization is sufficiently advanced. Again and again in entrance examinations and in second-year notebooks, I have found this idea expressed. It is not only the one thing which survives out of the essay, but is often the one conviction in regard to literature which has survived examinations as the result of the study of the entire entrance requirement. In the entrance paper of the Massachusetts Institute of Technology for last year (1905), I had put a question in regard to the difference between poetry and prose. From the replies I have taken a few of the many echoes from the study of the "Milton."

---

1    Since this was written this essay has been removed from the list, but the effects of it are still with us, as it was used for all classes entering college before 1906. I leave this comment, however, because of its important bearing on a point which I wish to bring up later.

> Macaulay claims that the uncivilized alone care for poetry.
>
> I agree with Macaulay that prose is the product of civilization, . . . while poetry was the way the ancients expressed themselves.
>
> Poetry is not being written nearly so much now as in the Dark Ages, simply because men are learning to treat subjects in classes.
>
> Macaulay says that the writer of a great poem must have a certain unsoundness of mind, and Carlyle makes the statement that to be a great poet a man must first be as a little child. If these opinions are just, one would think poetry could not be regarded as of a quality equal to prose works.
>
> Poetry came first in the lapse of time, and as people grew more civilized, as their education grew higher, they wrote in prose.

Obviously these extracts hardly do justice to the views of Macaulay, but it is evidently absurd to try to interest pupils in poetry when they are getting from one of the works selected "for careful study" the idea that the poet is a semi-madman practicing one of the habits of a half-civilized race![2]

Fortunately much of the reading is better, although in effect the books are sometimes limited by the difficulty of keeping the interest of children up for the long poem. The inclusion in the list of "Elaine" and "The Lady of the Lake" of course presupposes on the part of the pupil familiarity in the lower grades with lyrics and brief narrative poems; and in many cases this may be sufficient. Most pupils will be sure to care for "The Ancient Mariner," many for "The Princess;" and any wholesome boy, with ordinary intelligence, should be interested in "Ivanhoe" and "Macbeth."

As things stand, however, the teacher is forced to deal largely with books which almost compel formal and pedantic treatment. Burke's

---

2   See page 212.

"Speech on Conciliation," admirable as it is in its place and way, will hardly give to a young student an insight into literature or a taste for imaginative work. The normal, average lad is likely, it seems to me, to be bored by "Silas Marner," or at least very mildly interested; and I confess frankly my inability to understand how youthful enthusiasm is to be aroused or more than youthful tolerance secured for Irving's "Life of Goldsmith" or Macaulay's "Life of Johnson." Plenty of pupils are docile enough to allow themselves to be led placidly through these works, and indeed to submit to any volume imposed by school regulations; but what the teacher is endeavoring to do is to convince the young readers that books entitled to the name "literature" are really of more worth and interest than the newspaper, the detective story, the sensational novel, or the dime-theatre song. It is perhaps not possible to find among the English Classics works well adapted to such use,—although I refuse to believe it,—but I do at least feel that the present entrance-requirement list does not lend itself readily, to say the least, to the task of the teacher who aims at developing an intelligent and loving appreciation of literature.

The list of obstacles which beset the way of a teacher of literature might easily be lengthened; but these seem chief. They are discouraging; but they exist. They must be faced and overcome, and nothing is gained by ignoring them. The successful teacher, like the successful general, is he who most clearly examines difficulties, and best succeeds in devising means by which they may be vanquished.

# IV

# Other Obstacles

The difficulties set down in the last chapter exist in the conditions under which teachers must work. They should be recognized, to the end that they may be as far as possible overcome. They can be done away with only by the slow and gradual changing of public opinion and the re-forming of pedagogic intelligence. For the present they are to be reckoned with as inevitable limitations.

Another class of obstacles to the ideal result of the teaching of literature exists largely in the application of the modern system or in the method of the individual teacher. These may to a great extent be done away with by a proper understanding of conditions, a just estimate of what may be accomplished, and a wise choice of the means of doing this. Teachers must take things as they find them, but the ultimate result of work depends to a great extent upon how they take them. If they must often accept unfortunate conditions, they may at least reduce to a minimum whatever is uneffective in their own method.

The most serious defects which depend largely upon individual teaching are four. The first is the danger, already alluded to, of teaching children *about* literature; the second is that of making too great a demand upon the child; the third is the common habit of endeavoring to reach the enthusiasm of the pupil through the reason, instead of aiming at the reason through the enthusiasm; and the fourth is—to speak boldly— the possible incapacity of the teacher for this particular work.

The first of these is the most widespread. It is so natural to bring forward facts concerning the history of writers and of books, it is indeed so impossible to avoid this entirely; to induce students to repeat glibly what some critic has written about authors and their works is so easy, that this insensibly and almost inevitably tends to make up the bulk of instruction. Every incompetent teacher takes refuge in such formal drill. The history of literature is concrete; it is easily tabulated; and it is naturally accepted by children as being exactly in line with the work which properly belongs to other studies with which they are acquainted. If a child is set to treat literature just as he has treated history or mathematics, the process will appeal to him as logical and easily to be mastered. He will find no incongruity in applying the same method to "Macbeth" and to the list of Presidents or to the multiplication-table; and however well or ill he succeed in memorizing what is given him, he will feel the ease of working in accustomed lines. Names and dates may be learned by rote, old entrance-paper questions are tangible things, and thus examinations come to mean annual offerings of childish brains. To teach literature requires sympathy and imagination: the history of literature requires only perseverance. Much that in school reports is set down as the study of masterpieces is in reality only a mixture of courses in biography and history, more or less spiced with gossip.

The second danger, that of making too great a demand upon the child, is one which, to some extent, besets all school work to-day, but which seems to be especially great and especially disastrous in the case of the study we are considering. Often the nature of the questions asked shows one form of this demand in a way that is nothing less than preposterous. Children in secondary schools are required to have original ideas in regard to the character of Lady Macbeth; to define the workings of the mind of Shylock; to produce personal opinions in the discussion of the madness of Hamlet. Children whose highest acquirements in English composition do not and cannot reach beyond the plainest expository statement of simple facts and ideas, are coolly requested to discriminate between the style of "Il Penseroso" and that of "L'Allegro," and to show how each is adapted to the purpose of the poet. If they were allowed to write from the point of view of a child, the matter would be bad enough; but no teacher who sets such a task would be satisfied with anything properly belonging to the child-mind. It is probably safe to be tolerably certain that no teacher ever gave out this sort of a question who could without cribbing from the critics perform satisfactorily the task laid upon the unfortunate children.

I have before me a pamphlet entitled "Suggestions for Teachers of English Classics in the High Schools." It is not a gracious task to find fault with a fellow worker and a fellow writer in the same line in which I am myself offering suggestions, and I therefore simply put it to the common sense of teachers what the effect upon the average high school pupil would be if he were confronted with questions such as are included in the proposed outline for the study of "Evangeline." The author of the pamphlet directs that these points are to be used "after some power of analysis has been developed."

> The language.
>> Relative proportion of English and Latin.
>> Archaic element, proportion and use.
>> Weight of the style; presentative and symbolic words.
>> Emotional element; experimental significance of terms.
>> Picture-element; prevailing character of figures of speech.
> The structure.
>> Grammatical.
>>> Poetic uses of words; archaisms, poetic forms.
>>> Poetic uses of parts of speech, parse.[3]

---

3   I am unable to resist the temptation to call attention to the intimation that the writer perceives some relation between poetry and parsing. It would be interesting if he had developed this.

Poetic constructions and inversions, analyze.

Metrical.

Number and character of metrical "feet."

Accent and quantity, the spondee.

Scan selected lines, compare with classic hexameter.

Compare hexameter with other verse-forms.

Character of rhyme, compare with other poems.

Presence and use of alliteration.

Musical.

Examine for lightness and speed; trochee, dactyl, polysyllables.

Examine for dignity; iambus, monosyllables.

Number of syllables in individual lines.

Character of consonants; stopped, unstopped, voiced.

Character of vowels; back, front, round, harsh.

Correspondence of sound to sense.

It would be interesting, and perhaps somewhat humiliating, for each one of us who are teachers to take a list of the questions we have set for examinations in literature and with perfect honesty tell ourselves how many of them we could ourselves answer with any originality, and how many it is fair to suppose that our students could write about with any ideas except those gathered from teacher or text-book. With the pressure of a doubtful system and of unintelligent custom always upon us, few of us, it is to be feared, would escape without a sore conscience.

When I speak of a school-boy or a school-girl as writing with "originality," I do not mean anything profound. I am not so deluded as to suppose this originality will take the form of startlingly novel discoveries in regard to the significance of work or the intention of authors. I only mean that what the boy or girl writes shall be written because he or she really thinks it, and that each idea, no matter if it be obvious and crude, shall have some trace of individuality which will indicate that it has passed through the mind of the particular pupil who expresses it. This, I believe, is what should chiefly concern the maker of examination-papers. He should especially aim at giving students an opportunity of showing personal opinions and convictions.

No one who has looked over files of examination-papers is likely to deny that we are most of us likely to be betrayed into asking of our classes absurd things in the line of criticism. It is all very well to remember the scriptural phrase about the high character of some of the utterances of babes and sucklings; but this is hardly sufficient warrant for insisting that our school-children shall babble in philosophy and chatter in criticism. The honest truth is that we are constantly demanding of pupils things that we could for the most part do but very poorly ourselves. The unfortunate youngsters who should be solacing themselves with fairy-tales or with stories of adventure as their taste happens to be, are being dragged through "The Vicar of Wakefield,"—an exquisite book, which I doubt if one person in fifty can read to-day with proper appreciation and delight until he is at least twenty-five. They are being asked to write themes about Lady Macbeth,—and if they were really frank, and wrote their own real thoughts, if they considered her from the point of view of the children they are, where is the teacher who would not feel obliged to return the theme as a failure? Those instructors who recognized that it was of real worth because genuine would also realize that it would be impossible when tried by the modern standard of examinations.

How far individual teachers go in demanding from children what the youthful mind cannot be fairly expected to give will depend upon the personal equation of the instructor. In too many cases the entrance-examinations set a standard which in the fitting-schools may not safely be ignored, but which is fatal to all original thinking. Perhaps the worst form of this is the wrenching from the student what are supposed to be criticisms upon artistic form or content. A hint of the teaching which is intended to lead up to this has been given in the topics suggested in connection with the study of "Evangeline" on page 42. The "outline" from which those are quoted goes on to give the  following questions:

Of what literary spirit is "Evangeline" the expression?

What is the author's thought-habit as shown in the poem?

What is the place of this poem in the development of verse?

I am perhaps a little uncharitable to these queries because I am, I confess, entirely unable to answer them myself; but I am also sure that no child in the stage of mental development belonging to the secondary schools would have any clear and reasonable idea even of what they mean. The example is an extreme one, but it has more parallels than would seem possible.

The formulation of views on æsthetics, whether in regard to workmanship or to motive, is utterly beyond the range of any mental condition the teacher in secondary schools has a right to assume or to expect. All that can happen is that the student who is asked to answer æsthetic conundrums will reproduce, in form more or less distorted according to the parrot-like fidelity of his memory, views he has heard without understanding them. Any teacher of common sense knows this, and any teacher of independent mind will refuse to be bullied by manuals or by entrance-examination papers into inflicting tasks of this sort upon his pupils.

In any branch many students either go on blunderingly or fail altogether through sheer ignorance of how to study. In the case of literature perhaps more fail through this cause than through all others combined. A robust, honest, and not unintelligent lad, who is fairly well disposed toward school work, but whose real interests are in outdoor life and active sport, who is intellectually interested only in the obviously practical side of knowledge, is set down to "study" a play of Shakespeare's. He is disposed to do it well, if not from any vital interest in the matter, at least from a general habit of being faithful in his work and a healthful instinct to do a thing thoroughly if he undertakes it at all. He is at the outset puzzled to know what is expected of him. In arithmetic or algebra he has had definite tasks, and success has been in direct proportion to the diligence with which he has followed a course definitely marked out. Now he casts about for a rule of procedure. He can understand that he is expected to learn the meaning of unusual or obsolete words, that he is to make himself acquainted with the story so that he may be able to answer any of the conundrums which adorn ingeniously the puzzle department of examination papers. These things he does, but he is too sensible not to know that if this is all there is to the study of literature the game is not worth the candle. He cannot help feeling that the time thus employed might be put to a better use; he is probably bored; and as he is sure to know that he is bored, he is likely to conceive a contempt for literature which is none the less deep and none the less permanent for not being put into words. He very likely comes to believe, with the inevitable tendency of youth to make its own feelings the criteria by which to judge all the world, that everybody is really bored by literature, if only, for some inscrutable reason, people did not feel it necessary to shroud the matter in so much humbug. Talk about the beauty of Shakespeare, about the greatness of his poetry, the wonders of literary art, come to affect him as cant pure and simple. He puts this to himself plainly or not according to his temperament; but the feeling is in his mind, showing at every turn to one wise enough to discern. Now and then a boy is born with the taste and appreciation of poetry, and of course even in these days, when a literary atmosphere in the home is unhappily so rare, an occasional student appears from time to time who has been taught to care for poetry where every child should learn to love it, in the nursery. On the whole, however, the average school-boy really cares little or nothing for literature, and in his secret heart is entirely convinced that nobody else cares either.

Not knowing how to "study" literature, then, and feeling that in literature is nothing to study which is of consequence, the pupil is in no position to make even a reasonable beginning. He cannot even approach literature in any proper attitude unless he can be made to care for it; unless he can be so interested that he ceases to feel the profession of admiration for the Shakespeare he is asked to work upon to be necessarily cant and affectation. Perhaps the hardest part of the task set before the teacher is to bring the pupil into a frame of mind where he can properly study poetry and to give him some insight into what such study may and should mean.

How this is to be accomplished I cannot pretend fully to say. In speaking of what I may call "inspirational" training in literature I shall try to answer the question to some extent; and here I may at least point out that the situation is from the first utterly hopeless if the teacher is in the same state of mind as the pupil. If the instructor is able to see no method of studying literature other than mechanical drudgery over form, the looking-up of words, verification of dates, dissection of plot, and so on, it is idle to hope that he will be able to aid the class to anything better than this dry-as-dust plodding. The teacher may at least learn what at its best the "study" is. He may or may not have the power of inciting those under him to enthusiasm, but he may at least show them that something is possible beyond the mechanical treatment of the masterpieces of art.

A writer in the (Chicago) "Dial" states admirably the attitude of great masses of students in saying:

> There are many people, young people in particular, who, with the best will in the world, cannot understand why it is that men make such a fuss about literature, and who are honestly puzzled by the praises bestowed upon the great literary artists. They would like to join in sympathetic appreciation of the masters, and they have an abundant store of gratitude and reverence to lavish upon objects that approve themselves as worthy; but just what there is in Shakespeare and

Wordsworth and Tennyson to call for such seeming extravagance of eulogy remains a dark mystery. Such people are apt in their moments of revolt to set it all down to a sort of critical conspiracy, and to consider those who voice the conventional literary estimates as chargeable with an irritating kind of hypocrisy. They cannot see for the life of them why the books of the hour, with their timeliness, their cleverness, their sentimental or sensational interest, should be held of no serious account by the real lovers of literature, while the dull babblers of a bygone age are exalted to the skies by these same devotees of the art of letters. . . . Some young people never recover from the condition of open revolt into which they are thrown by the injudicious methods of our education.

Out of his own experience and appreciation the teacher must be able to show the pupil some method of studying literature which shall in the measure of the student's individual capacity lead to a conception of what literature is and wherein lies its importance. Until this can be done, nothing has been effected which is of any real or lasting value.

The third defect which I have mentioned I have put in a phrase which may at first seem somewhat cryptic. What is meant by the attempt to reach the enthusiasm of the child through the reason may not be at once apparent. Yet the thing is simple. It is not difficult to lead children to think, and to think deeply, of things which have touched their feeling. If once their emotions are aroused, they will go actively forward in every investigation of which their minds are capable, and with whatever degree of appreciation they are equal to. A child cannot, however, be reasoned into any vital admiration. The extent to which an adult is to be touched emotionally by argument is extremely limited. Few travelers, for instance, are able really to respond when an officious verger or care-taker points out some historic spot, and after glibly relating some event in his professional patter, ends with a look which says almost more plainly than words:

"Stand just here, and thrill! Sixpence a thrill, please." Yet this is very much what is expected of children. The teacher takes a famous book, laboriously recounts its merits, its fame, its beauties, and then tacitly commands the children: "Think of that, and thrill! One credit for every thrill." It is true that the verger demands a fee and the teacher promises a reward, but the result is the same. Do the children thrill? Is there a conscientious teacher who has tried this method who has not with bitter disappointment realized that the students have come out of the course with nothing save a few poor facts and disfigured conventional opinions which they reserve for examinations as they might save battered pennies for the contribution-box? They have been personally conducted through a course of literature. They come out of it in much the same condition as return home the personally conducted through foreign art-galleries who say: "Yes, I must have seen the 'Mona Lisa,' if it's in the Louvre. I saw all the pictures there, you know." The chief difference is that children are generally incapable, outside of examination-papers, of pretending an enthusiasm which they do not feel.

One thing which is indisputable is that children know when they are bored. Many adults become so proficient in the art of self-deception as to be able to cheat themselves into thinking they are at the height of enjoyment because they are doing what they consider to be the proper thing; when in simple truth their only pleasure must lie in the gratification of a futile vanity. Of children this is seldom true; or, if it is true, it extends only to the fictions practiced by their own childish world. If they have conventions, these differ from the conventions of their elders, and they do not fool themselves with a show of enjoyment when the reality is wanting. If they are wearied by a book, the fact that it is a masterpiece does not in the least console them. They may be forced by teachers to read or to study it, and to say on examination-papers that it is beautiful; yet they not only know they are not pleased, but to each other they are generally ready to acknowledge it with perfect frankness.

The need of saying this in the present connection is that it is not possible really to convince children they are enjoying the writing of themes about Mrs. Primrose, or about Silas Marner and Effie, or on the character of Lady Macbeth, unless they are vitally interested. I am far from being so modern as to think that pupils should not be asked to do anything which they do not wish to do; but I am radical enough to believe that no other good which may be accomplished by the study of literature in any other way can compensate for making good books wearisome. The idea that literature is something to be vaguely respected but not to be read for enjoyment is already sufficiently prevalent; and rather than see it more widespread, I would have all the so-called teaching of literature in the secondary schools abolished altogether.

The last point which I mentioned as likely to diminish the value of teaching is that it so often demands of teachers more than can be surely or safely counted on in the way of fitness. This I do not mean to dwell upon, nor is it my purpose to draw up a bill of arraignment against my craft. I wish simply to comment that one essential, a prime essential, in the teaching of literature is the power of imaginative enthusiasm on the part of the teacher. This would be recognized if the subject of instruction were any other of the fine arts. If teachers were required to train school-children in the symphonies of Beethoven or in the pictures of Titian, everybody would realize that some special aptitude on the part of the instructor was requisite. Every normal school or college graduate is set to teach the masterpieces of Shakespeare or of Milton, and the fact that the poetry is as completely a work of art as is symphony or picture, and that what holds true of one as the product of artistic imagination must hold true of the other, is quietly and even unconsciously ignored.

No amount of study will create in a teacher the artistic imagination in its highest sense, although much may be done in the way of developing artistic perception; but at least self-improvement may go far in the nourishing of the important quality of self-honesty. An instructor must learn to deal fairly with himself. He must be strong enough to acknowledge to himself fearlessly if he is not able to care for some work that is ranked as an artistic masterpiece. He must be willing to say unflinchingly to himself that he cannot do justice to this work or to that, because he is not in sympathy with it, or because he lacks any experience which would give him a key to its mood and meaning.

One thing seems to me to be entirely above dispute in this delicate inquiry: that it is idle to hope to impart to children what we have not learned ourselves; and it follows that the first necessity is to appreciate our shortcomings. I ask only for the same sort of honesty which would by common consent be essential in teaching the more humble branches. A teacher who could not solve quadratic equations would manifestly be an ill instructor in algebra. By the same token it is evident that a teacher who cannot enter into the heart of a poem, who does not understand the mood of a play, who has not a real enthusiasm for literature, is not fitted to help children to a comprehension and an appreciation of these. Neither is the power to rehearse the praises and phrases of critics or commentators a sufficient qualification for teaching. In an examination-paper at the Institute of Technology a boy recently wrote with admirable frankness and directness:

> I confess that while I like Shakespeare, I like other poets better, and while my teachers have told me that he was the greatest writer, they never seemed to know why.

The boy unconsciously implies a most important fact, namely, that if a teacher does not know why a poet is great, it is not only difficult to convince the pupil of the reality of his claims, but also is it impossible to disguise from the clever scholars the real ignorance of the instructor. As well try to warm children by a description of a fire as to endeavor to awake in them admiration and pleasure by parrot-phrases, no matter how glibly or effectively repeated. They are aroused only by the contagion of genuine feeling; they are moved only by finding that the teacher is first genuinely moved himself.

It is bad enough when an instructor repeats unemotionally what he has unemotionally acquired about arithmetic or geography. Pupils will receive mechanically whatever is mechanically imparted; and in even the most purely intellectual branches such training can at best only distend the mind of the child without nourishing it. When it comes to a study which is presented as of value precisely because it kindles feeling, the absurdity becomes nothing less than monstrous.

Any child of ordinary intelligence comes sooner or later to perceive, whether he reasons it out or not, that much of the literature presented to him is not in the least worth the bother of study if it is to be taken merely on its face-value. If "The Vicar of Wakefield" or "Silas Marner" is to be read simply for the plot, either book might be swept out of existence to-morrow and the world be little poorer. A conscientious teacher will at least be honest with himself in determining how much more than the obvious and often slight face-value he is enabling his class to perceive.

An ordinary modern school-boy unconsciously but inevitably measures the values of the books presented to him by the news of the day and the facts of life as he sees it. If he is not made to feel that books represent something more than a statement of outward fact or of fiction, he is too clear-headed not to see that they are of little real worth, and with the pitiless candor of youth he is too honest not to acknowledge this to himself. Young people are apt to credit their elders with enormous power of pretending. The conventionalities of life, those arrangements which adults recognize as necessary to the comfort and even to the continuance of society, are not infrequently regarded by the young as rank hypocrisy. The same is true of any tastes which they cannot share. Again and again I have come upon the feeling among students that the respect for literature professed by their elders was only one of the many shams of which adult life appears to children to be so largely made up.

From the purely intellectual side of the matter, moreover, the youth is right in feeling that there is nothing so remarkable in play or poem as to justify the enthusiasm which he is told he should feel. If he sees only what I have called the face-value, he would be a dunce if he did not imagine an absurdity in the estimate at which the works of great artists are held. He is precisely in the position of the man who judges the great painting by its realistic fidelity to details, and logically, from his point of view, ranks a well-defined photograph above "The Night Watch" or the Dresden "Madonna." There is more thrill and more emotion for the boy in the poorest newspaper account of a game of football than in the greatest play of Shakespeare's,—unless the lad has really got into the spirit of the poetry.

If nothing is to be taken into account but the intellectual content of literature, the child is therefore perfectly right, and doubly so from his own point of view. Regarded as a mere statement of fact it is to be expected that the average modern boy will find "Macbeth" far less exciting and absorbing than an account of a football match or of President Roosevelt's spectacular hunting. If we expect the lad to believe without contention and without mental reservation that the work of literature is really of more importance and interest than these articles of the newspaper or the magazine, we are forced to depend upon the qualities which distinguish poetry as art. If books are to be used only as glove-stretchers to expand mechanically the minds of the young, it is better to throw aside the works of the masters, and to come down frankly to able expositions of literal fact, stirring and absorbing.

It must be always borne in mind, moreover, that little permanent result is produced except by what the pupil does for himself. The teacher is there to encourage, to stimulate, to direct; but the real work is done in the brain of the student. This limits what may wisely be attempted in the line of instruction. What the teacher is able to lead the pupil to discover or to think out for himself is within the limit of sound and valuable work. With every class, and—what makes the problem much more difficult—with every boy or girl in the class, the capacity will vary. The signs, moreover, by which we determine how far a child is thinking for himself, instead of more or less consciously mimicking the mind of the master, are all well-nigh intangible, and must be watched for with the nicest discernment. Often the teacher is obliged to help the class or the individual as we help little children playing at guessing-games with "Now you are hot," or "Now you are cold;" but just as the game is a failure if the child has in the end to be told outright the answer to the conundrum, so the instruction is a failure if the student does not make his own discovery of the meaning and worth of poem or play. The moment the instructor finds himself forced to do the thinking for his class in any branch of study, he may be sure that he has overstepped the boundary of real work, or at least that he has been going too rapidly for his pupils to keep pace with him. This is even likely to be true when he is obliged to do the phrasing, the putting of the thought into word. He cannot profitably go farther at that time. In another way, at another time, he may be able to bring the class over the difficulty; but he is doing them an injury and not a benefit, if he go on to do for them the thinking, or that realizing of thought which belongs to putting thought into word. He is then not educating, but "cramming." It is his duty to encourage, to assist, but never to do himself what to be of value must be the actual work of the learner himself.

All this is evident enough in those branches where results are definite and concrete, like the learning of the multiplication-table or of the facts of geography. It is equally true in subjects where reasoning is essential, like algebra or syntax. Most of all, if not most evidently, is it vitally true in any connection where are involved the feelings and anything of the nature of appreciation of artistic values. We evidently cannot do the children's memorizing for them; but no more can we do for them their reasoning; and least of all is it possible to manufacture for them their likings and their dislikings, their appreciations and their enthusiasms. To tell children what feelings they should have over a given piece of literature produces about the same effect as an adjuration to stop growing so fast or a request that they change the color of their eyes.

In any emotional as in any intellectual experience, intensity and completeness must ultimately depend upon the capacity and the temperament of the individual concerned. It is useless to hope that a dull, stolid, unimaginative boy will have either the same appreciation or the same enjoyment of art as his fellow of fine organization and sensitive temperament. The personal limitation must be accepted, just as is accepted the impossibility of making some youths proficient in geometry or physics. It may be necessary under our present system— and if so the fact is not to the credit of existing conditions—to present the dull pupil with a set of ideas which he may use in examinations. The proceeding would be not unlike providing the dead with an obolus by way of fare across the Styx; and certainly in no proper sense could be considered education. Difficult as it may be, the pupil must be made to think and to feel for himself, or the work is naught.

Perhaps the tendency to try to do for the student what he should accomplish for himself is the most general and the most serious of all the errors into which teachers are likely to fall. The temptation is so great, however, and the conditions so favorable to this sort of mistake, that it is not possible to mete out to instructors who fall into it an amount of blame at all equal to the gravity of the offense.

# V

# Foundations of Work

The foundation of any understanding or appreciation of literature is manifestly the power of reading it intelligently. A truth so obvious might seem to be taken for granted and to need no saying; but any one who has dealt with entrance examination-papers is aware how many students get to the close of their fitting-school life without having acquired the power of reading with anything even approaching intelligence. Primary as it may sound, I cannot help emphasizing as the foundation of all study of literature the training of students in reading, pure and simple.

The practical value of simple reading aloud seems to me to have been too often overlooked by teachers of literature. Teachers read to their pupils, and this is or should be of great importance; but the thing of which I am now speaking is the reading of the students to the teacher and to the class. In the first place a student cannot read aloud without making evident the degree of his intelligent comprehension of what he is reading. He must show how much he understands and how he understands it.

The queer freaks in misinterpretation which come out in the reading of pupils are often discouraging enough, but they are amusing and enlightening. Any teacher can furnish absurd illustrations, and it is not safe to assume of even apparently simple passages that the child understands them until he has proved it by intelligent reading aloud. The attention which oral reading is at present receiving is one of the encouraging signs of the times, and cannot but do much to forward the work of the teacher of literature.

Of so much importance is it, however, that the first impression of a class be good, that the instructor must be sure either to find a reasonably good reader among the pupils for the first rendering or must give it himself. In plays this is hardly wise or practicable; but here the parts are easily assigned beforehand, and the pride of the students made a help in securing good results. In any work a class should be made to understand that the first thing to do in studying a piece of literature is to learn to read it aloud intelligently and as if it were the personal utterance of the reader.

In dealing with a class it is often a saving of time and an easy method of avoiding the effects of individual shyness to have the pupils read in concert. In dealing with short pieces of verse this is, moreover, a means of getting all the class into the spirit of the piece. The method lacks, of course, in nicety; but it is in many cases practically serviceable.

Above everything the teacher must be sure, before any attempt is made to do anything further, that the pupil has a clear understanding at least of the language of what he reads. My own experience with boys who come from secondary schools even of good grade has shown me that they not infrequently display an extraordinary incapability of getting from the sentences and phrases of literature the most plain and obvious meaning, especially in the case of verse; while as to unusual expressions they are constantly at sea. On a recent entrance examination-paper I had put, as a test of this very power, the lines from "Macbeth:"

And with some sweet oblivious antidote

Cleanse the stuff'd bosom of that perilous stuff.

The play is one which they had studied carefully at school, and they were asked to explain the force in these lines of "oblivious."

Here are some of the replies:

> "Oblivious," used in this quotation, means that the person speaking was not particular as to the kind of antidote that was chosen.

> A remedy that would not expose the lady to public suspicion.

> The word "oblivious" implies a soothing cure, which will heal without arousing the senses.

> An antidote applied in a forgetful way, or unknown to the person.

> "Oblivious" here means some antidote that would put Lady Macbeth to sleep while the doctor removed the cause of the trouble.

> "Oblivious antidote" means one that is very pleasing.

> The word "oblivious" is beautifully used here. Macbeth wishes the doctor to administer to Lady Macbeth some antidote which will cure her of her fatal [*sic*] illness, but which will not at all be any bitter medicine.

> "Oblivious" here means relieving.

> "Oblivious" means some remedy the doctor had forgotten, but might remember if he thought hard enough.

Of course many of the replies were sensible and sound, but those hardly better than these were discouragingly numerous.

In my own second-year work, in which the students have had all the fitting-school training and the freshman drill besides, I am not infrequently confounded by the inability of students to understand the meaning of words which one uses as a matter of course. The statement that Raleigh secretly married a Lady in Waiting, for instance, reappeared in a note-book in the assertion that Sir Walter ran away with Queen Elizabeth's waiting-maid; and a remark about something which took place at Holland House brought out the unbelievable perversion that the event happened "in a Dutch tavern." Personally I have never discovered how far beyond words of one syllable a lecturer to students may safely go in any assurance that his language will be understood by all the members of his class; but this is one of the things which must be decided if teaching is to be effective.

It must always be remembered that the vocabulary of literature is to some extent different from that employed in the ordinary business of life. The student is confronted with a set of terms which he seldom or never uses in common speech; he must learn to appreciate fine distinctions in the use of language; he must receive from words a precision and a force of meaning, a richness of suggestion, which is to be appreciated only by special and specific training. It will be instructive for the teacher to take any ordinary high-school class, for instance, and examine how far each member gets a complete and lucid notion of what Burke meant in the opening sentence of the "Speech on Conciliation:"

> I hope, Sir, that notwithstanding the austerity of the Chair, your good nature will incline you to some degree of indulgence toward human frailty.

An instructor is apt to assume that the intent of a passage such as this is entirely clear, yet I apprehend that not one high-school pupil in twenty gets the real force of this unaided.

If this example seems in its diction too remote from every-day speech to be a fair example, the teacher may try the experiment with the sentence in "Books" in which Emerson speaks of volumes that are

> So medicinal, so stringent, so revolutionary, so authoritative.

Every word is of common, habitual use, but most young people would be well-nigh helpless when confronted with them in this passage.

The use in literature of allusion, of figures, of striking and unusual employment of words, must become familiar to the student before he is in a condition to deal with literature easily and with full intelligence. The process must be almost like that of learning to read in a foreign tongue. For a teacher to ignore this fact is to take the position of a professor in Italian or Spanish who begins the reading of his pupils not with words and simple sentences, but with intricate prose and verse.

It must be remembered, moreover, that if the diction of literature is removed from the daily experience of the pupil, the ideas and the sentiments of literature are yet more widely apart from it. Literature must deal largely with abstract thoughts and ideas, expressed or implied; it is necessarily concerned with sentiments more elevated or more profound than those with which life makes the young familiar. They must be educated to take the point of view of the author, to rise to the mental plane of a great writer as far as they are capable of so doing. Until they can in some measure accomplish this, they are not even capable of reading the literature they are supposed to study.

Fortunately it is with reading literature as it is with reading foreign tongues. Often the context, the general tone, the spirit, will carry us over passages in which there is much that is not clear to our exact knowledge. Children are constantly able to get from a story or a poem much more than would seem possible to their ignorance of the language of literature. They are helped by truth to life even when they are far from realizing what they are receiving; so that it would be manifestly unjust to assume that the measure of a child's profit in a given case is to be gauged too nicely by his acquaintance with the words, the phrases, the tropes, the suggestions in which the author has conveyed it. The fact remains, however, that in attempting to do anything effective in the way of instruction the teacher has first of all to train his pupil in the language of literature.

The student, having learned to read the work which is to be studied, must approach it through some personal experience. The teacher who is endeavoring to assist him must therefore discover what in the child's range of knowledge may best serve as a point of departure. In all education, no less than in formal argument, a start can be made only from a point of agreement, from something as evident to the student as it is to the instructor. Consciously or unconsciously every teacher acts upon this principle, from the early lessons in addition which begin with the obvious agreement produced by the sight of the blocks or apples or beads which are before the child. In literature, too, the fact is commonly acted upon, if not so universally formulated. If young pupils are having "The Village Blacksmith" read to them, the teacher instinctively starts with the fact that they may have seen a blacksmith at work at his forge. The difficulty is that teachers who naturally do this in simple poems fail to see that the same principle holds good of literature of a higher order, and that the more complex the problem, the greater the need of being sure of this beginning with some actual experience.

With this finding some safe and substantial foundation in the pupil's own experience is connected the necessity of speaking of literature, as of anything else one tries to teach, in the language of the class addressed. Of all that we say to our pupils very little if any of all our careful wisdom really impresses them or remains in their minds except that portion which we have managed to phrase in terms of their language and so to put that it appeals to emotions of their own young lives. They can have no conception of the characters in fiction or poetry except in so far as they are able to consider these shadows as moving in their own world. They should be told to make up their minds about Lady Macbeth, or Robin Hood, or Dr. Primrose as if these were persons of their own community about whom they had learned the facts set forth in the books read. They cannot completely realize this, but they get hold of the fictitious character only so far as they are able to do it. They will at least come to have a conception that people they see in the flesh and those they meet in literature are of the same stuff fundamentally, and should be judged by the same laws. They will receive the benefit, moreover, whether they realize it or not, of being helped by fiction to understand real life, and they will be in the right way of judging books by experience.

The principle of speaking to pupils only in the language of their own experience is of universal application, but it is to be applied with common sense. Nothing is more unfortunate in teaching than to have pupils feel that they are being talked down to or that too great an effort is being made to bring instruction to their level. A friend once told me of a professor who in the days of the first period of tennis enthusiasm in this country made so great an effort to take all his illustrations from the game that the class regarded the matter a standing joke. Yet if care be exercised it is not difficult to mix with the childish, the familiar, and the commonplace, the dignified, the unusual, and the suggestive. Starting with a daily experience the teacher may go on to states of the same emotion which are far greater and higher than can have come into the actual life of the child, but which are imaginatively intelligible and possible because although they differ in degree they are the same in kind. Nothing is lost of the dignity of a play of Shakespeare's dealing with ambition if the teacher starts with ambition to be at the head of the school, to lead the baseball nine, or to excel in any sport; but from this the child should be led on through whatever instances he may know in history, and in the end made to feel that the ambition of Macbeth is an emotion he has felt, even though it is that emotion carried to its highest terms. So the small and the great are linked together, and the use of the little does not appear undignified because it has been a stepping-stone to the great.

The aim in teaching literature is to make it a part of the student's intimate and actual life; a warm, human, personal matter, and not a thing taken up formally and laid aside as soon as outside pressure is removed. To this end is the appeal made to the pupil's experience, and to this end is he allowed to make his own estimates, to formulate his own likes and dislikes. Any teacher, it must be remembered, is for the scholar in the position of a special pleader. The student regards it as part of the pedagogic duty to praise whatever is taught, and instinctively distrusts commendation which he feels may be only formal and official. He forms his own opinion independently or from the judgment of his peers,—the conclusions of his classmates. He may repeat glibly for purposes of recitation or of examination the criticisms of the teacher, but he is likely to be little influenced by them unless they are confirmed by the voice of his fellows and his own taste. If young people do not reason this out, they are never uninfluenced by it; and this condition of things must be accepted by the teacher.

It follows that it is practically never wise to praise a book beforehand. The proper position in presenting to the class any work for study is that it is something which the class are to read together with a view of discovering what it is like. Of course the teacher assumes that it has merit or it would not be taken up, but he also assumes that individually the members of the class may or may not care for it. The logical and safe method is to set the students to see if they can discover why good judges have regarded the work as of merit. The teacher should say in effect: "I do not know whether you will care for this or not; but I hope you will be able to see what there is in it to have made it notable."

When the study of poem or play is practically over, when the pupils have done all that can be reasonably expected of them in the way of independent judgment, the teacher may show as many reasons for praising it as he feels the pupils will understand. He must, however, be honest in letting them like it or not. He must recognize that it is better for a lad honestly to be bored by every masterpiece of literature in existence than to stultify his mind by the reception of merely conventional opinions got by rote.

Much the same thing might be said of the drawing of a moral, except that it is not easy to speak with patience of those often well-meaning but gravely mistaken pedagogues who seem bound to impress upon their scholars that literature is didactic. In so far as a book is deliberately didactic, it is not literature. It may be artistic in spite of its enforcing a deliberate lesson, but never because of this. My own instinct would be, and I am consistent enough to make it pretty generally my practice, to conceal from a class as well as I can any deliberate drawing of morals into which a writer of genius may have fallen. It is like the fault of a friend, and is to be screened from the public as far as honesty will permit. Certainly it should never be paraded before the young, who will not reason about the matter, but are too wholesome by nature and too near to primitive human conditions not to distrust an offering of intellectual jelly which obviously contains a moral pill.

Morals are as a rule drawn by teachers who feel that they must teach something, and something tangible. They themselves lack the conception of any office of art higher than moralizing, and they deal with literature accordingly. They are unable to appreciate the fact that the most effective influence which can be brought to bear upon the human mind is never the direct teaching of the preacher or the moralizer, but the indirect instruction of events and emotions. Personally I have sufficient modesty, moreover, to make me hesitate to assume that I can judge better than a master artist how far it is well to go in drawing a moral. If the man of genius has chosen not to point to a deliberate lesson, I am far from feeling inclined to take the ground that I know better, and that the sermon should be there. When Shakespeare, or Coleridge, or Browning feels that a vivid transcript of life should be left to work out its own effect, far from me be the presumption to consider the poet wrong, or to try to piece out his magnificent work with trite moralizing.

The tendency to abuse children with morals is as vicious as it is widespread. It is perhaps not unconnected with the idea that instruction and improvement must alike come through means not in themselves enjoyable. It is the principle upon which an old New England country wife rates the efficacy of a drug by its bitterness. We all find it hard to realize that as far as literature, at least, is concerned, the good it does is to be measured rather by the pleasure it gives. If the children entirely and intelligently delight in it, we need bother about no morals, we need—as far as the question of its value in the training of the child's mind goes—have no concern about examinations. Art is the ministry of joy, and literature is art or it is the most futile and foolish thing ever introduced into the training of the young.

# VI

# Preliminary Work

It will not always do to plunge at once into a given piece of literature, for often a certain amount of preliminary work is needed to prepare the mind of the pupil to receive the effect intended by the author. For convenience I should divide the teaching of literature into four stages:

- Preliminary;
- Inspirational;
- Educational;
- Examinational.

The division is of course arbitrary, but it is after all one which comes naturally enough in actual work. One division will not infrequently pass into another, and no one could be so foolish as to suppose literature is to be taught by a cut and dried mechanical process of any sort. The division is convenient, however, at least for purposes of discussion; and no argument should be needed to prove that in many cases the pupil cannot even read intelligently the literature he is supposed to study until he has had some preparatory instruction.

The vocabulary of any particular work must first be taken into account. We do not ask a child to read a poem until we suppose him to have by every-day use become familiar with the common words it contains. We should remember that the poet in writing has assumed that the reader is equally familiar with any less common words which may be used. It is certainly not to be held that the writer intends that in the middle of a flowing line or at a point where the emotion is at its highest, the reader shall be bothered by ignorance of the meaning of a term; that he shall be obliged to turn to notes to look up definitions, shall be plunged into a puddle of derivations, allied meanings, and parallel passages such as are so often prepared by the ingenious editors of school texts. These things are well enough in their place and way; but no author ever intended his work to be read by any such process, and since literature depends so largely on the production of a mood, such interruptions are nothing less than fatal to the effect.

I remember as a boy sitting at the feet of an elder sister who was reading to me in English from a French text. At the very climax of the tale, when the heroine was being pursued down a wild ravine by a bandit, the reader came to an adjective which she could not translate. With true New England conscientiousness she began to look it up in the dictionary; but I could not bear the delay. I caught the lexicon out of her hands, and without having even seen the French or knowing a syllable of that language, cried out: "Oh, I know that word! It means 'blood-boltered.' Did he catch her?" She abandoned the search, and in all the horror of the picturesque Shakespearean epithet the bandit dashed on, to be encountered by the hero at the next turn of the romantic ravine. I had at the moment, so far as I can remember, no consideration of the exact truth of my statement. I simply could not bear that the emotion of the crisis should be interrupted by that bothersome search for an exact equivalent. The term 'blood-boltered' fitted the situation admirably, and I thrust it in, so that we might hurry forward on the rushing current of excitement. This, as I understand it, is the fashion in which children should take literature. Few occasions, perhaps, are likely to call for epithets so lurid as that in which Macbeth described the ghost of Banquo, but the spirit of the thing read should so carry the reader forward that he cannot endure interruption.

When work must be done with glossary and notes in order that the text may be easily and properly understood, this should be taken as straightforward preliminary study. It should be made as agreeable as possible, but agreeable for and in itself. When I say agreeable for itself, I mean without especial reference to the text for which preparation is being made. The history of words, the growth and modification of meanings, the peculiarities and relations of speech, may always be made attractive to an intelligent class; and since here and throughout all study of literature students are to be made to do as much of the actual work as possible, this part is simple.

The amount of time given to such learning of the vocabulary might at first seem to be an objection to the method. In the first place, however, there is an actual economy of time in doing all this at first and at once, thus getting it out of the way, and saving the waste of constant interruptions in going over the text; in the second, it affords a means of making this portion of the work actually interesting in itself and valuable for its relation to the study of language in general; and in the third place it both fixes meanings in mind and allows the reading of the author with some sense of the effect he designed to give by the words he employed.

It is hardly necessary to say that in this matter of taking up the vocabulary beforehand many teachers, perhaps even most teachers, will not agree with me. The other side of the question is very well put in a leaflet by Miss Mary E. Litchfield, published by the New England Association of Teachers in English:

> My pupils, I find, can work longer and harder on "Macbeth" and "Hamlet," with constantly increasing interest, than on any other masterpieces suited to school use. Just because these dramas are so stimulating, the pupils have the patience to struggle with the difficulties of the text. In general they feel only a languid interest in word-puzzles such as delight the student of language; for instance, the expression, "He doesn't know a hawk from a handsaw," might fail to arouse their curiosity. But when Hamlet says: "I am but mad north-north west: when the wind is southerly I know a hawk from a handsaw," they are on the alert; they really care to know what he means and why he has used this peculiar expression. Thus word-

study which might be mere drudgery is rendered interesting by the human element in the play—the element which, in my opinion, should always be kept well in the foreground.

A large number of teachers, many of them, very likely, of experience greater than mine, will agree with this view. I am not able to do so because I believe we should know the language before we try to read; but I at least hold that the first principle in any successful teaching is that a teacher shall follow the method which he finds best adapted to his own temperament. For the instructor who is convinced that the habit of taking up difficulties of language as they are met in actual reading, to take them up then is perhaps the only effective way of doing things. It seems to me, however, a little like sacrificing the literature to a desire to make teaching the vocabulary easier. It is very likely a simpler way of arousing interest in difficulties of language; but in teaching literature the elucidation of obscure words and phrases is of interest or value simply for the sake of the effect of the text, and I hold that to this effect, and to this effect as a whole, everything else should be subordinate. Each teacher must decide for himself what is the proper method, but I insist that no author ever wrote sincerely without assuming that his vocabulary was familiar to his audience beforehand. Certainly I am not able to feel that it is wise to interrupt any first reading with anything save perhaps the briefest possible explanations, comments that are so short as not to break the flow of the work as a whole.

The first reading of a narrative of any sort, it may surely be said, is chiefly a matter of making the reader, and especially the childish reader, acquainted with the story. Since little real study can be accomplished while interest is concentrated on the plot, it may be wise for the teacher to have a first reading without any more attention to the difficulties of vocabulary than is absolutely needed to make the story intelligible, and then to have the difficulties learned before a second and more intelligent going over of the work as a whole. Each teacher must decide a point of this sort according to individual judgment and the character of the class.

In all the lower grades of school work whatever literature is given to the children should be in diction and in phrasing so simple that very little of this sort of preliminary work need be done. So long as what is selected has real literary excellence it can hardly be too simple. We constantly forget, it seems to me, how simple is the world of children. Dr. John Brown, dear and wise soul, has justly said:

> Children are long in seeing, or at least in looking at what is above them; they like the ground, and its flowers and stones, its "red sodgers" and lady-birds, and all its queer things; *their world is about three feet high*, and they are more often stooping than gazing up.

It does not follow that children are to be fed on that sort of water-gruel which is so often vended as "juvenile literature." They should be given the best, the work of real writers; but of this the simplest should be chosen, and in dealing with it the children should not be bothered with thoughts and ideas which are over their heads. They live, it must be remembered, in a "world about three feet high," mentally as well as physically.

In preliminary work the first object is to remove whatever obstacles might hinder ease and smoothness of progress in reading. Beside having all obscure terms understood, it is well to call attention to some of the most striking and beautiful passages in the book or poem which is to be read. They should be taken up as detached quotations, and the pupils made to discover or to see how and why each is good. The pleasure of coming upon them when the text is read helps in itself; it diminishes the strain upon the mind of the student in the effort of comprehension, and it doubles the effect of the portions chosen. My idea is that many fine passages may be treated almost as a part of the vocabulary of the text; their meaning and force may be made so evident and so attractive that when the complete play or poem is taken up a knowledge of these bits helps greatly in securing a strong effect of the work as a whole.

We teachers too often ignore, it is to be feared, the strain it is to the young to understand and to feel at the same time. We fail to recognize, indeed, how difficult it is for them—or for any one—to *feel* while the attention is taxed to take in the meaning of a thing; so that in literary study we are likely to demand the impossible, the responsiveness of the emotions while all the force of the child's mind is concentrated upon the effort to comprehend. Whatever may be done legitimately to lessen this stress is most desirable. The preparation of the vocabulary, the elucidation of obscure passages obviously aids in this; but so does the pointing out of beauties. Instead of being bothered in the midst of the effort to take in a poem or a play as a whole and being harassed by the need of mastering details of diction or phrasing, the student has a pleasant sense of self-confidence in coming upon obscure matters already conquered; and in the same way receives both pleasure and a feeling of mastery in recognizing beauties already familiar.

The preliminary work, besides this study of any difficulties of vocabulary, should include whatever is needful in making clear any difference between the point of view of the work studied and that of the child's ordinary life.

In "The Merchant of Venice," for instance, it is necessary to make clear the fact that the play was written for an audience to which usury was an intolerable crime and a Jew a creature to be thoroughly detested. The Jew-baiting of recent years in Europe helps to make this intelligible. The point must be made, because otherwise Antonio appears like a cad and Jessica inexcusable. The story is easily brought home to the school-boy, moreover, by its close relation to the simplest emotions.

The two facts that Antonio has incurred the hatred of Shylock through his kindness to persons in trouble and that he comes within the range of danger through raising money to aid his friend Bassanio are so closely allied to universal human feelings and universal human experience that it is only needful to be sure these points are clearly perceived to have the sympathies of the class thoroughly awakened.

All this is so obvious that it is hardly necessary to say it except for the sake of not omitting what is of so much real importance. Every teacher understands this and acts upon it.

To include this in the preliminary work may seem a contradiction of a previous statement that it is not wise to tell children what they are expected to get from any given book. The two matters are entirely distinct. What should be done is really that sort of giving of the point of view which we so commonly and so naturally exercise in telling an anecdote in conversation. "Of all conceited men I ever met," we say, "Tom Brandywine was the worst. Why, once I saw him"—and so on for the story which is thus declared to be an exposition of overweening vanity. "See," we say to the class in effect, "you must have felt sorry to see some kindly, honest fellow cheated just because he was too honest to suspect the sneak that cheated him. Here is the story of a great, splendid, honest Moor, a noble general and a fine leader, who was utterly ruined and brought to his death in just that way." This is not drawing a moral, and it seems to me entirely legitimate aid to the student. It is less doing anything for them that they could and should do than it is directing them so that they may advance more quickly and in the right direction.

This indication of the general direction in which the mind should move in considering a work is closely connected with what might be called establishing the proper point of departure. This is neither more nor less than fixing the fact of common experience in the life of the pupil at which it seems safe and wise to begin. What has been said about the way in which a teacher calls upon the experience of the pupils to bring home the picture of the Village Blacksmith at his forge is an indication of what is here meant. In teaching history to-day, with a somewhat older grade of pupils than would be reading that poem of Longfellow's, an instructor naturally makes vivid the Massacre of St. Bartholomew by comparison with the reports of Jewish massacres in our own time; and in the same line the fact that it is so short a time since the King of Servia was assassinated, or that the present Sultan of Turkey cemented on his crown with the blood of his brothers, may be made to assist a class to take the point of view necessary for the realization of the tragedy in "Macbeth." I have already spoken[4] of the humbler, but perhaps even more vital way in which the vice of ambition that is so strong a motive power in that tragedy is to be understood by starting from the rivalry in sports, since from this so surely intelligible emotion the mind of the boy is easily led on to the ambition which burns to rule a kingdom. It is wise not to be afraid of the simple. If the poem to be studied is "The Ancient Mariner," it is well to discover what is the strangest situation in which any member of the class has ever found himself. After inciting the rest of the pupils to imagine what must be one's feelings in such circumstances, it is not difficult to lead them on to understand the declaration of Coleridge that he tried to show how a man would feel if the supernatural were actual.

For natural, wholesome-minded children it is not in the least necessary to take pains to reconcile them to the supernatural. To the normal child the line between the actual and the unreal does not exist until this has been drilled into him by adult teaching, conscious or unconscious. The normal condition of youth is that which accepts a fairy as simply and as unquestioningly as it accepts a tree or a cow. Certainly it is true that children are in general ready enough for what they would call "make-believe," that stage of half-conscious self-deception which lies between the blessed imaginative faith of unsophisticated childhood and the more skeptical attitude of those who have discovered that "there isn't any Santa Claus." For all younger classes nothing more is likely to be necessary than to assume that the wonderful will be accepted.

When occasion arises to justify the marvellous, the teacher may always call attention to the fact that in poems like "The Ancient Mariner," or "Comus," or "Macbeth" the supernatural is a part of the hypothesis. To connect with this the pupil's conception of the part the hypothesis plays in a proposition in geometry is at once to help

4   Page 69.

to connect one branch of study with another, always a desirable thing in education, and to aid them in understanding why and how they are to accept the wonders of the story entirely without question. The impossible is part of the proposition, and this they must be made to feel before they can be at ease with their author or get at all the proper point of view.

The aim of literature is to arouse emotion, but we live in a realistic age, and the youth of the present is not given to the emotional. Youth, moreover, instinctively conceals feeling, and the lads in our school-classes to-day are in their outside lives and indeed in most of their school-work called upon to be as hard-headed and as unemotional as possible. They are likely to feel that emotion is weak, that to be moved is effeminate. They will shy at any statement that they should feel what they read. The notion of conceiving an hypothesis helps just here. A boy will accept—not entirely reasoning the thing out, but really making of it an excuse to himself for being moved—the idea that if the hypothesis were true he might feel deeply, although he assures himself that as it is he is actually stable in a manly indifference. The aim of the teacher is to awake feeling, but not to speak of it; to touch the class as deeply as possible, yet not to seem aware, or at least not to show that he is aware that the students are touched.

In this as in all treatment of literature, any connection with the actual life of the pupil is of the greatest value. It seems to justify emotion, and it gives to the work of imagination a certain solidity. Without reasoning the thing out fully, a boy of the present day is likely to judge the importance of anything presented to him at school by what he can see of its direct bearing upon his future work, and especially by its relations to the material side of life. This is even measurably true of children so young that they might be supposed still to be ignorant of the realism of the time and of the practical side of existence. The teacher best evades this danger by starting directly from some thought or fact in the child's present life and from this leading him on to the mood of the work of literature which is under consideration.

Here and everywhere I feel the danger of seeming to be recommending mechanical processes for that which no mechanical process can reach. If the teacher has a sympathetic love for literature, he will understand that I do not and cannot mean anything of the sort; if he has not that sympathy, he cannot treat literature otherwise than in a machine fashion, no matter what is said. It sometimes seems that it is hardly logical to expect every teacher to be an instructor in literature any more than it would be to ask every teacher to take classes in music and painting. Art requires not only knowledge but temperament; both master and pupil must have a responsiveness to the imaginative, or little can be accomplished. Since the exigencies of our present system, however, require that so large a proportion of teachers shall make the attempt, I am simply endeavoring to give practical hints which may aid in the work; but I wish to keep plainly evident the fact that nowhere do I mean to imply a patent process, a mechanical method, or anything which is of value except as it is applied with a full comprehension that the chief thing, the thing to which any method is to be at need completely sacrificed, is to awaken appreciation and enthusiasm, to quicken the imagination of the student, and to develop whatever natural powers he may have for the enjoying and the loving of good books.[5]

---

5 While this volume was in press a writer in the *Monthly Review* (London) has remarked: «I fail to see how a literary sense can be cultivated until a firm foundation of knowledge has been laid whereon to build, and I tremble to think of the result of an enforced diet of ‹The Canterbury Tales,› ‹The Faerie Queen,› and ‹Marmion› upon a class as yet ignorant of the elements of English composition.»

# VII

# The Inspirational Use of Literature

The term "inspirational," which I have used as indicating the second division of the teaching of literature, is a somewhat absurdly large word for what is the most simple and natural part of the whole dealing with books which goes on between teacher and pupil. It is a term, however, which expresses pretty well what is or should be the exact character of the study at its best. The chief effect of literature should be to inspire, and by "inspirational," as applied to teaching, I mean that presentation of literature which best secures this end.

Put in simpler terms the whole matter might be expressed by saying that the most important office of literature in the school as in life is to minister to delight and to enthusiasm; and whoever is familiar with the limited extent to which the required training in college requirements or in prescribed courses fulfils this office will realize the need which exists for the emphasizing of this view of the matter. Literature is made a gymnasium for the training of the intellect or a treadmill for the exercise of the memory, but it is too seldom that delight which it must be to accomplish its highest uses.

That the secondary schools should be chiefly concerned with this phase of literature seems to me a truth so obvious and so indisputable that I can see only with astonishment that it is so generally ignored. In the lower grades, it is true, something is done in the way of letting children enjoy literature without bothering about didactic meanings, history of authors, philological instances, critical manipulations, and all the devices with which later the masterpieces of genius are turned into bugbears; but even here too many teachers feel an innate craving to draw morals and to make poetry instructive. They seem to forget that as children themselves they skipped the moral when they read a story, or at best received it as an uninteresting necessity, like the core of an apple, to be discarded when from it had been gleaned all the sweets of the tale. Nothing is more amazing than the extent to which all we teachers, in varying degrees, but universally, even to the best of us, go on dealing with a sort of imaginary child which from our own experience we know never did and never could exist. The first great secret of all teaching is to recognize that we must deal with our pupils as if we were dealing with our own selves at their age. If we can accomplish this, we shall not bore them with dull moralizings under the pretext that we are introducing them to the delights of literature.

Where a class has to be dealt with, the work in any branch must be adapted to the average mind, and not to the understanding of the individual; so that in school many things are impossible which at home, or in individual training, are not difficult. It is not hard, I believe, to interest even the average modern boy, distracted by the multiplicity of current impressions, in the best literature, provided he may be taken alone and competently handled. Almost any wholesome and sane lad may at times be found to be indifferent in class to the plays of Shakespeare, for instance; yet I believe few healthy and fairly intelligent boys of from ten to fifteen could resist the fascination of the plays if these were read with them by a competent person at proper times, and without the dilution of mental perception which necessarily comes with the presence of classmates. Be this, however, as it may, the teacher must be content with arousing as well as he can the spirit of the class as a whole. Some one or two of the cleverest pupils will lead, and may seem to represent the spirit of all; but even they are not what they would be alone, and in any case the instructor must not devote himself to the most clever while the rest of the pupils are neglected.

It follows that in the choice of pieces to be read to students the first thing to be considered is that these shall be effective in a broad sense so that they will appeal to the average intelligence and taste of a given class easily and naturally. They must first of all have that strong appeal to general human emotion which will insure a ready response from youth not well developed æsthetically and rendered less sensitive by being massed with other students in a class. Such a selection is not easy, and it involves the careful study of what may be termed the individuality of any given group of pupils; but it seems to me to be at once one of the most obvious and one of the most important of the points which should be considered in the beginning of any attempt to create in school a real enjoyment in literature.

A danger which naturally presents itself at the very outset is the likelihood of forgetting that the possession of this easy and obvious interest is not a sufficient reason why a work should be presented to a class. It too often happens that the desire of arousing and interesting pupils leads teachers to bring forward things that are sensational and have little if any further recommendation. Doubtless Dr. Johnson was right when he declared that "you have done a great thing when you have brought a boy to have entertainment from a book;" yet after all the teacher is not advancing in his task and may be doing positive harm if he sacrifice too much to the desire to be instantly and strongly pleasing. Flashy and unworthy books are so pressed upon the reading public at the present day that especial care is needed to avoid fostering the tendency to receive them in place of literature.

It is not my purpose to give lists of selections, for in the first place it has been done over and over, notably in such a collection as the admirable "Heart of Oak" series; and in the second no selection can be held to be equally adapted to different classes or to have real value unless it has been made with a view to the actual needs of a definite body of pupils. Pupils must be interested, yet the things chosen to arouse their interest should be those which have not only the superficial qualities which make an instant appeal, but possess also those more lasting merits essential to genuine literature.

In the lower grades it is generally, I believe, possible for the teacher to control the choice of selections put before students, although even here this is not always the case. If errors of selection are made, however, they are largely due to inability to judge wisely and to a too great deference to general literary taste. A teacher must remember that two points are absolutely essential to any good teaching of literature: first, that the selection be suited to the possibilities of the individual class; second, that the teacher be qualified so to use and present the selection as to make it effective. Many conscientious teachers take poems which they know are regarded as of high merit, and which have been used with advantage by other instructors, yet which they individually, from temperament or from training, are utterly inadequate to handle. They either lack the insight and delight in the pieces which are essential if the pupils are to be kindled, or are deficient in power so to present their own appreciation and enjoyment that these appeal to the children.

For illustration of one of the ways in which a child may be led into the heart of a poem I have chosen "The Tiger," by William Blake. This belongs to the class of literature constantly taken for use with children because it is reputed to be beautiful, yet which constantly fails in its appeal to a class. It is to me one of the most wonderful lyrics in the language, yet I doubt if it would ever have occurred to me to use it in our common schools, and certainly I should never have dreamed that it was to be presented to children in the lower grades. I do not know with what success teachers in general may have used it, but in one or two Boston schools with which I happen to be fairly well acquainted the effect is pretty justly represented by the mental attitude of the small lad spoken of in the next chapter. The extent to which children acquiesce in a sort of mechanical compliance in what to them are the vagaries of their elders in the matter of literature can hardly be exaggerated. Doubtless they often unconsciously gain much of which they do not dream in the way of the development of taste and perception, but too often the whole of the instruction given along æsthetic lines slides over them without producing any permanent effect of appreciable value.

Of course I do not contend that children are not advancing unless they know it. Early training in literature may often be of the highest value without definite consciousness on the part of the child. Self-analysis is no more to be expected here than anywhere else in the early stages of training. The child does not in the least comprehend, for instance, that the ditties of Mother Goose, meaningless jingles as they are, are educating his sense of rhythm; he does not understand that his imaginative powers are being nourished by the fairy-tale, the normal mental food for a certain stage of the development of the individual as it is the natural and inevitable product of a corresponding stage in the development of the race. So long as a child has genuine interest in a poem or a tale he is getting something from it, but he does not concern himself to consider anything beyond present enjoyment. In the earlier stages at least, and for that matter at any stage, the thing to be secured is interest; and instruction in the lower school grades should be confined to what is actually needed to make children enjoy a given piece. Anything beyond this may wisely be deferred.

In many of the lower grades it is now the fashion to have children act out poems. The method is spoken of with satisfaction by teachers who have tried it. I know nothing of it by experience, but should suppose it might be good if not carried too far. Children are naturally histrionic, and advantage may be taken of this fact to stimulate their imagination and to quicken their responsiveness to literature, if seriousness and sincerity are not forgotten.

In this early work it does not seem to me that much can wisely be done in the study of metrical effects. Indeed, I have serious doubts whether much in the way of the examination of the technique of poetry properly has place anywhere in preparatory schools. The child, however, should be trained gradually to notice metrical effects, by having attention called to passages which are especially musical or impressive. By beginning with ringing and strongly marked verse and leading on to effects more delicate the teacher may do much in this line.

I have called this early work "inspirational" because it should be directed to making literature a pleasure and an inspiration. The word, clumsy as it may seem, does express the real function of art, and the only function which may with any profit be considered in the earlier stages of the "study" of literature. The object is to make the children care for good books; to show them that poetry has a meaning for them; and to awaken in them—although they will be far from understanding the fact—a sensitiveness to ideals. The child will not be aware that he is being given higher views of life, that he is being trained to some perception of nobler aims and possibilities greater than are presented by common experiences; but this is what is really being accomplished. Any training which opens the eyes to the finer side of life is in the best and truest sense inspiration; and it should be the distinct aim of the teacher to see to it that whatever else may happen, in the lower grades or in the higher, this chief function of the teaching of literature shall not be lost sight of or neglected.

# VIII

# An Illustration

To attempt to give a concrete illustration of the method in which any teaching is to be carried on is in a way to try for the impossible. Every class and every pupil must be treated according to the especial nature of the case and the personal equation of the teacher. I perhaps expose myself to the danger of seeming egotistic if I insert here an experience of my own, and, what is of more consequence, I may possibly obscure the very points I am endeavoring to make clear. As well as I can, however, I shall set down an actual talk, in the hope that it may afford some hint of the way in which even difficult pieces of literature may be made to appeal to a child. Of course this is not in the least meant as a model, but solely and simply as an illustration.

"Do you like it?" I asked.

"Oh, we don't have to like it," he responded with careless frankness, "we just have to learn it."

The form of his reply appealed to one's sense of humor, and I wondered how many of my own students in literature might have given answers not dissimilar in spirit, had they not outgrown the delicious candor which belongs to the first decade of a lad's life. The afternoon chanced to be rainy and at my disposal. I was curious to see what I could do with this combination of Blake and small boy, and I made the experiment. I should not have chosen the poem for one so young; but it is real, compact of noble imagination, the boy was evidently genuine, and a real poem must have something for any sincere reader even if he be a child.

The following report of our talk was not written down at the time, and makes no pretense of being literal. It does represent, so far as I can judge, with substantial accuracy what passed between the straightforward lad and myself. Too deliberate and too diffuse to have taken place in a school-room, it yet gives, on an extended scale, what I believe is the true method of "teaching literature" in all the secondary-school work. I do not claim to have originated or to have discovered the method; but I hope that I may be able to make clearer to some teachers how children may be helped to do their own thinking and thus brought to a vital and delighted enjoyment of the masterpieces they study.

I began to repeat aloud the opening lines of the poem.

"Why," said the boy, "do you know that? Did you have to learn it at school when you were little like me?"

"I'm not sure when I did learn it," I answered; "I've known it for a good while; but I didn't just learn it. I like it."

I repeated the whole poem, purposely refraining from giving it very great force, even in the supreme symphonic outburst of the magnificent fifth stanza:

> Tiger, tiger, burning bright
>
> In the forests of the night,
>
> What immortal hand or eye
>
> Could frame thy fearful symmetry?
>
> In what distant deeps or skies
>
> Burnt the fire of thine eyes?
>
> On what wings dare he aspire?
>
> What the hand dare seize the fire?

And what shoulder and what art

Could twist the sinews of thy heart?

And, when thy heart began to beat,

What dread hand formed thy dread feet?


What the hammer? what the chain?

In what furnace was thy brain?

What the anvil? what dread grasp

Dare its deadly terrors clasp?


When the stars threw down their spears,

And watered heaven with their tears,

Did he smile His work to see?

Did he who made the lamb make thee?

"It sounds rather pretty," I commented, as carelessly as possible.

"Yes, I suppose so," he assented colorlessly, looking at me rather suspiciously.

He was a shrewd little mortal, and he had been so often told at school that he should like this and that for which in reality he did not care a button that he was on his guard. I made a casual remark about something entirely unrelated to the subject. It was well that the lad should not feel that he was being instructed. Then in a manner as natural and easy as I could make it I asked:

"Did you ever see a tiger?"

"Oh, yes; I've seen lots of them at the circus. Tom Bently never went to but one circus, but I've been to four."

"What does a tiger look like?" I went on, ignoring the irrelevant.

"He's a fierce-looking thing! Didn't you ever see one?"

"Yes, I've seen them, but I wondered if they looked the same to you as they do to me."

"Why, how do they look to you?"

"I asked you first. It's only fair for you to say first."

"Well," the small boy said, with a fine show of being determined to play fair, "I think they look like great big, big, big cats. Did you think that?"

"That's exactly what I should have said. They really are a sort of cat, you know. Did you ever see a keeper stir them up?"

"Oh, yes, sir; and they snarled like anything, and licked their lips just like this!"

He gave a highly gratifying imitation, and then added vivaciously: "If I were the keeper, I'd keep stirring them up all the time. They did look so mad!"

"And they opened and shut their eyes slowly," I suggested, "as if they'd like to get hold of their keeper."

"Yes; and their eyes were just like green fire."

"'Burning bright,'" I quoted; and then without giving the boy time to suspect that he was being led on, I asked at once: "Did you ever see a cat's eyes in the dark?"

"Oh, I saw our cat once last summer, when we were in the country, under a rosebush after dark, when Dick and I got out of the window after we'd gone to bed. She just scared me; her eyes were just like little green lanterns. Dick said they were like little bicycle lamps."

"If it had been a tiger under a bush in the night,—'in the forests of the night,›—»

"Oh," interrupted the boy with the eagerness of a discoverer, "is that what it means! Did he see a tiger in the night under a bush? A real, truly tiger, all loose? I'd have run away."

"I don't know if he ever saw one," I answered. "I rather think he saw a tiger or a picture of one, or thought of one, and then got to thinking how it must seem to come across one in the woods; when one was travelling, say, in the East where tigers live wild. If you came upon one in the forest in the dark, what do you think would be the first thing that would tell you a tiger was near?"

"I'd hear him."

"Did you ever hear a cat moving about?"

"No," the boy said doubtfully. "Aunt Katie says Spot doesn't make any more noise than a sunbeam. Could a sunbeam make a noise?"

"She meant that Spot didn't make any. You'd never hear a tiger coming, for it's a kind of cat, and moves without sound. You wouldn't know that way."

"I'd see him."

"In the night? You couldn't see him."

"Yes, I could! Yes, I could!" he cried triumphantly. "I'd see his eyes just like green fire."

I had interested the lad and taken him far enough to feel sure he would follow me if I helped him on a little faster. I was ready to use clear suggestion when I felt that he would respond to it as if the thought were his own.

"Well," I said, "don't you see that this is just what the man who wrote the poem meant? He got to thinking how the tiger would look in the night to anybody that came on him in the forest and saw those eyes like green fires shining at him out of the jungle. Don't you suppose you or I would think they were pretty big fires if we saw them, and knew there was a tiger behind them?"

"I guess we should! Wooh! Do you suppose Bruno'd run?"

Bruno was a small and silky water-spaniel, a charming beast in his way, but not especially welcome at this point of the conversation.

"Very likely;" I slid over the subject. "The man knew that he would have a feeling how big and strong that tiger must be: and it gave him a shock to think what a fearful thing the beast would be there in the dark, with all the warm, damp smells of the plants in the air, and the strange noises. It would almost take away his breath to think what a mighty Being it must have taken to make anything so awful as a tiger."

"Yes," the lad said so quietly that I let him think a little. He had snuggled up against my knee and laid hold of my fingers, and I knew some sense of the matter was working in him. After a moment or two I asked him if he could repeat the first verse of the poem as if he were the man who thought of the tiger in the jungle there, with fierce eyes shining out of the dark, and who had so clear an idea of the mighty creature that he couldn't help thinking what a wonderful thing it was that it could be created. The boy fixed his eyes on mine as if he were getting moved and half-consciously desired to be assured that I was utterly serious and sympathetic; and in his clear childish voice he repeated in a way that had really something of a thrill in it:

"Tiger, tiger, burning bright

In the forests of the night,

What immortal hand or eye

Could frame thy fearful symmetry?"

"If a traveller were in the jungle in the dark night," I went on after a word of praise for his recitation, "I suppose he couldn't see much around him, the trees would be so thick. He'd have to look up to the sky to see anything but the tiger's eyes."

"He'd see the stars there," the boy observed, just as I had hoped he would. "I've seen stars through the trees. I was out in the woods long after dark once."

"Were you really? The man must have thought the stars looked like the eyes, as if when the animal was made the Creator went to the sky itself for that fire. Think of a Being that could rise to the very stars and take their light in His hand."

"Ouf!" the small man cried naïvely. "I shouldn't want to take fire in my hand!"

"The writer of the poem was thinking what a wonderful Being He must be that could do it; but that if He could make a creature like the tiger, He would be able to do anything."

The boy reflected a moment, and then, with a frank look, asked: "Did the fire in a tiger's eyes really come out of the stars?"

"I don't think that the poem means that it really did," was my answer. "I think it means that when the poet thought how wonderful a tiger is, with the life and the fierceness shining like a flame in his eyes, and how we cannot tell where that fire came from, and that the stars overhead were scarcely brighter, it seemed as if that was where the green light came from. He was trying to say how wonderful and terrible it was to him,—especially when he thought of coming upon the beast all alone in the forest in the night with nobody near to defend him."

The boy was silent, and thinking hard. He had evidently not yet clearly grasped all the idea.

"But God didn't make a tiger on an anvil and put pieces of stars in for eyes," he objected.

"You told me yesterday that Bruno swims like a duck. He doesn't really, for a duck goes on the top of the water."

"Oh, but I meant that Bruno goes as fast as a duck."

"And you wanted me to know how well he swims, I suppose."

"Why, of course. Bruno can swim twice as fast as Tom Talcott's dog."

"You said that about the duck to make me know what a wonderful swimmer Bruno is, and the man who wrote the poem wanted you when you read it to feel how wonderful the tiger seemed to him; its eyes as if they were of fire brought from the stars, its strength so great that it seemed as if his muscles had been beaten out on an anvil from red-hot steel by some Being mighty enough to do something no man could begin to do. The poem doesn't mean that a tiger was really made in this way; but it does mean that when you think of the strength and fearfulness of the creature, able to carry off a man or even a horse in its jaws, this is the best way to give an idea of how terrible the animal seemed."

The boy accepted this, and so we came to the fifth verse. The range of ideas here is so much beyond the mind of any child that it was necessary to suggest most of them, to go very slowly, and in the end to be content with a childishly inadequate notion of the magnificent conception. I gave frankly a suggestion of the creation of all the animals at the beginning, and of how the angels might have stood around like stars, watching full of interest and of kindness. The boy was easily made to feel as if he had seen the making of the deer and the lamb and the horse, and of how the angels might see in one or another of the animals a help or a friend to man.

"Then suppose," I said, "that the angels should see God make the great tiger, royal and terrible. What would they see?"

"Oh, a great fierce thing," the lad returned. "Do you suppose he'd jump right at the deer and the lambs?"

"He would make the angels think how he could. How different from the other animals he'd be."

"Yes, he'd have big, big, sharp teeth, and he'd lash his tail, and he'd put out his claws. Do you suppose he'd sharpen his claws the way Muff does on the leather chairs?"

"Very likely he would," I said. "At any rate the angels would think how the other animals would be torn to pieces if the tiger got hold of them; and they would think of what would happen to men. Perhaps they would imagine some poor Hindu woman, with her baby on her back going through a path in the jungle, and how the tiger might leap out suddenly and tear them both to pieces. The angels couldn't understand how God could bear to make any animal so cruel, or how He could be willing to have anything so wicked in the world. They would be so sorry for all the suffering that was to come that they would throw down their spears and not be able to keep back the tears."

"But angels wouldn't have spears, would they?"

I went to a shelf of the library in which we were talking and took down a volume in which I found a picture of St. Michael in full armor.

"It is like the fire from the stars," I said. "Of course nobody ever saw an angel to know how he would look, but to show how strong and powerful an angel might be, a good many men that make pictures have painted them like knights."

"But men that had spears wouldn't cry; I shouldn't think angels would."

"Even the strongest men cry sometimes, my boy; only it has to be something tremendous to make them. A thing that would make the angels 'water heaven with their tears' must be something so terrible that you couldn't tell how sad it was."

"Well, anyway, I'd rather be a tiger than a lamb," he proclaimed rather unexpectedly.

"Very likely," I assented, "but I think you'd rather have a lamb come after Baby Lou than a tiger."

"Oh, I wouldn't want a tiger to get Baby Lou!" he cried with a tremor.

"I suppose that is the way the angels might feel at the idea of the tiger's killing anybody," I rejoined.

With a lad somewhat older one would have gone on to develop the thought that to the watching angels the tiger, leaping out fierce and bloodthirsty from the hand of the Creator, would be like the incarnation of evil, and that in their weeping was represented all the sorrowful problem of the existence of evil in the Universe; but this on the present occasion I did not touch upon.

"So the angels," I went on, "couldn't keep back their tears; but what did God do?"

"Why, He smiled!" the boy answered, evidently with astonishment at the thought which now for the first time came home to him. "I shouldn't think He'd have smiled."

"When you were so disappointed the other day because the carriage was broken and you couldn't go over to the lake in it, do you remember that Uncle Jo laughed?"

"Oh, he knew we could go in his automobile."

"He knew."

"Yes, he knew," began the boy, "and so—" He stopped, and looked at me with a sudden soberness. "What did God know?" he asked seriously.

"He must have known that somehow everything was right, don't you think? He knew why He had made the tiger, just as He knew why He had made the lamb, and so He could see that everything would be as it should be in the end."

"But—but—"

The boy was speechless in face of the eternal problem, as so many greater and wiser have been before him. It seemed to me that we had done quite enough for once, so I broke off the talk with a suggestion that we try the boy's favorite game. That was the end of the matter for the time, but in the library of the lad's father the copy of Blake is so befingered at the page on which "The Tiger" is printed that it is evident that the boy, with the soiled fingers of his age, has turned it often. How much he made out of the talk I cannot pretend to say, but at least he came to love the poem.

I said at the start that I do not give the conversation, which is actual, as a sample, but as an illustration. The poem called for more leading on of the pupil than would many, for as Blake is one of the most imaginative of English writers, his conceptions are the more subtle and profound. A class, moreover, cannot be treated always with the same deliberation as that which is natural in the case of a single child; but the essential principle, I believe, is the same everywhere.

# IX

# Educational

Educational in the broadest sense must anything be which is inspirational; for to interest the child in literature, to make him enter into it as into a charming heritage, is more truly to educate him than would be any pedantic or formal instruction whatever. I have used the term specifically, however, as a convenient word by which to designate that form of instruction which is more deliberately and formally an effort to make clear what literature may be held to teach. To regard any work of art as directly and didactically teaching anything is perhaps to fail in so far to treat it as art; but the point which such a consideration raises is too deep for our present inquiry, and may be disregarded except in the case of unintelligent attempts to make every tale or poem embody and convey a set moral. To endeavor to aid pupils to perceive fully the relation of what they read to themselves and to the society in which they live is part of the legitimate work of the teacher of literature. In a word, while the term is perhaps not the best, I have used the word educational to designate such study as is directed to helping the student to gain from books a wider knowledge of life and human nature.

It is not my idea that in actual practice a formal division is to be made, and still less that what I have called inspirational consideration of literature is ever to be discontinued. In the growth of a child's mind comes naturally a simple and unreflecting pleasure in literature, beginning, as has been said, with unsophisticated delight in the marked rhythms of Mother Goose or in the wholesome joy of the fairy-story. To this is gradually added an equally unreflecting absorption of certain ideas concerning life, which by slow degrees gives place to reflection conscious and deliberate. The delight and the unconscious yielding to the influence of the work of art remain, and to the end they are more effective than any deliberate and conscious ideas can be. Nothing that we teach our pupils about a poem can compare in influence with what they absorb without realizing what they are doing. One of the great dangers of this whole matter is that we shall hurry them from an instinctive to a cultivated attitude toward literature; that we shall replace natural and healthful pleasure by laborious and conscientious study. In dealing with any piece of real literature the wise method, it seems to me, is to take it up first for the absolute, straightforward emotional enjoyment.[6] It is of very little use to study any work which the children have not first come to care for. After they see why a piece is worth while from the point of view of pleasure, then study may go further and consider what is the core of the work intellectually and emotionally.

In speaking of treating literature educationally I do not refer to that sort of instruction which so generally and unfortunately takes the place of the true study of masterpieces. The history of a poem or a drama, the biography of authors, and all work of this sort should in any case be kept subordinate and should generally, I believe, come after the student has at least a tolerable idea and a fair appreciation of the writings themselves. What is important and what I mean by the educational treatment of literature is the development of those general truths concerning human nature and human feeling which form the tangible thought of a play or poem. The line of distinction between this and the less tangible ideas which are conveyed by form, by melody, by suggestion,—the ideas, in short, which are the secret of the inspirational effect of a work,—cannot be sharply drawn. Many of the tangible ideas will have been obvious in the reading of which the recognized purpose has been mere delight and inspiration; and

---

6   The vocabulary, of course, being known before the text is attempted.

on the other hand the two classes of ideas are so closely interwoven that it is not possible, even were it advisable, to separate them entirely. It is possible, however, after the pupil has come to take pleasure in a work,—though it should never be attempted sooner,—to go on to the deliberate study of the intellectual content, and to take up broad and general truths.

One way of preparing a class for the work which is now to be done is to speak to them of literature as a sort of high kind of algebra; to let them see, that is, how the distinction between the great mass of reading-matter and what is fairly to be called literature is not unlike the difference with which they are familiar in mathematics between arithmetic and the higher grade of work which comes after. The newspaper, the text-book, the history, the scientific treatise all deal with the concrete, just as arithmetic has to do with absolute quantities. In the mental development of the pupil the time comes when he is considered sufficiently advanced to go on from the handling of concrete things to the dealing with the abstract. When he is able to understand the relation between the sum paid for one bushel of wheat and the amount needed to purchase fifty, he may be advanced to the lore of general formulæ, and be made to understand how $x$ may represent any price and $y$ any number of bushels. In the same way from reading in a newspaper the story of the assassination of the late King of Servia, the concrete case, he may go on to read "Macbeth," wherein Duncan represents any monarch of given character, and Macbeth not a particular, actual, concrete assassin, but a murderer of a sort, a type, the general or abstract character. The student has gone on from the particular to the general; from the concrete to the abstract; from the arithmetic of human nature to its algebra.

A similar comparison between history and poetry is on the same grounds easily to be made between the history lesson and the chronicle plays of Shakespeare. The student who in his nursery days started out with the instinctive question in regard to the fairy-tale:

"Is it true?" begins to perceive the difference between literal and essential truth. He perceives that verity in literature is not simple and obvious fidelity to the specific fact or event; he learns to appreciate that the truth of art, like the truth of algebra, lies in its accuracy in representing truth in the abstract: he comes to appreciate the narrowness of the nursery question, which asked only for the literal fact, and he begins to comprehend something of the symbolic.

An excellent illustration for practical use is a poem like "How they Brought the Good News from Ghent to Aix." Any live, wholesome boy is sure to tingle with the swing and fervor of the verse, the sense of the open air, the excitement, the doubt, the hope, the joyful climax. It is easy to lead the class on to consider how exhilarating such an experience would be, and to go on from this to point out that the poem does not describe a literal, actual occurrence; but that it is a generalized expression of the zest and exhilaration of a superb, all but impossible ride, with the added excitement of being responsible for the freedom or even the lives of the folk of a whole city.

The first feeling of the class on learning that such a ride was not taken is sure to be one of disappointment. It is better to meet this frankly, and to compensate for it by arousing interest in the embodiment of abstract feeling. One great source of the lack of interest in literature at the present time is that the material, practical character of the age makes it difficult for the general reader to respect anything but the concrete fact. Literature is apt to present itself to the hard-headed young fellow of the public school as a lot of make-believe stuff, and therefore at best a matter of rather frivolous amusement. The surest way of correcting this common attitude of mind is to nourish the appreciation of what fact in art really means; to cultivate a clear perception of how a poem or a tale may be the truest thing in the world, although dealing with imaginary personages and with incidents which never happened.[7]

---

7   See page 221.

As an illustration of the sense in which literature is a sort of algebra of human feeling somewhat more remote from the ordinary life of a child may be taken another poem of Browning's, "The Lost Leader." My experience is that most youth of the school age start out by being able to make little or nothing of this. By a little talk, however, beginning perhaps as simply as with the way in which a lad feels when a school-fellow he had faith in has failed in a crisis, has for some personal advantage gone over to the other party in a school election, or of how the class would feel if some teacher who had been with the students in some effort to obtain an extension of privilege to which the scholars felt themselves to be honestly entitled had for his own purposes swung over to the opposite side, the whole thing may be brought home. The boys may be led on to imagine what are the feelings of a youth eager for the cause of freedom and the uplifting of man, when one whom he has looked to as a leader, one in whom he has had absolute faith, deserts the rank for honors or for money. Once the young minds are on the right track it is by no means impossible to bring them to see pretty clearly that in the poem is not the question of a particular man or a particular cause; but that Browning is dealing with a universal expression of the pain that would come to any man, to any one of them, in believing that the leader who had been most trusted and revered had in reality been unworthy, and had betrayed the cause his followers believed he would gladly die to defend.

These two examples from Browning I have taken almost at random, and not because they are unusual in this respect, for this quality is the universal property of all real literature, and indeed is one of the tests by which real literature is to be identified. Any selection which it is worth while to give students at all must have this relation which I have called "algebraic," but of which the true name is imaginative; and it is certainly one of the important parts of anything which in a high sense is properly to be called "teaching" literature to make the scholars realize and appreciate this.

The next step is more difficult because far more subtle; and I confess frankly that it is all but impossible to propose methods by which formal instruction may deal with it. The aim of literature is largely the attempt to produce a mood. The prime aim of the poet is to induce in the reader a state of feeling which will lead inevitably to the reception of whatever he offers in the same mood in which he offers it. In the simplest cases no instruction is needed, for even with school-boys a ringing metre, to take a simple and obvious example, has somewhat the same effect as the dashing swing of martial music; whoever comes under its influence falls insensibly into the frame of mind in which the ideas of the verse should be received. The thoughts are accepted in the exhilarated spirit in which they were written, and the effects of the metre are as great or greater than the influence of the literal meaning. It is a commonplace to call attention to the part which the melody of poetry or the rhythm of prose plays in the effect, but how to aid pupils to a responsiveness to this language of form is not the least of the problems of the teacher.

The means by which an author establishes or communicates his mood do not always appeal to the young. Indeed, beyond a certain limited extent they appeal to most adults only after careful cultivation in the understanding of art-language. It is as idle to suppose that literature appeals to everybody and without æsthetic education as it is to suppose that sculpture or music will surely meet with a response everywhere. Nobody expects Beethoven's "Ninth Symphony" or Bach's "Passion Music" to arouse enthusiasm in accidentally assorted school-children, yet to all the pupils in a mixed public school are offered the parallel works of Shakespeare and Milton. Unless a class is made up of boys or girls with unusual aptitude or wisely and carefully trained to responsiveness to metrical effect, it seems hardly less idle to offer them "Comus" or "Lycidas" than it would be to expect them to enjoy a classic concert. The language of form in the higher range of literature is to them an unknown tongue.

Children are likely to be susceptible to marked metrical effects, as witness their love of "Mother Goose;" but to the more delicate music of verse they are often largely or completely insensitive. A musical ear is not, it is probable, to be created, but it is certainly possible to develop the metrical sense. Children who are born with good native responsiveness to rhythm often are so badly trained or so neglected as to seem to have none, and it is part of the office of instruction to call out whatever powers lie in them latent. This is largely accomplished by the sort of use of literature which I have called "inspirational." In the ideal home-training children are so taken on from the rhymes of the nursery to more advanced literature that development of the rhythmical sense is continuous and inevitable; but one of the things which every school-teacher knows best is that this sort of home-training is rare and the work must be done in the class. The substitute is a poor one, but it has at least some degree of the universal human responsiveness to rhythm to appeal to.

Another difficulty is that children have to learn the verbal language of literature. Much of the atmosphere of a poem, for instance, is likely to be produced by suggestion, by the mention of legend or tale or hero, when the reader must find in previous knowledge and association a key to what is intended. All this is likely to be largely or entirely lost on children; and yet this is often the very quintessence of what the author tries to convey. Children are constantly at the same disadvantage in understanding literature that they are in comprehending life. They have not gathered the associations or experienced the emotions which make so large a part of the language of great writers. All this renders it difficult for the instructor to be sure that his class has any inkling even of the mood in which a piece is intended; yet he must first of all be sure that as far as is possible he has put them, each pupil according to his character and acquirements, in touch with the spirit of the work to be studied.

This cannot be done entirely. We cannot hope that a lad of a dozen years will enter into all the emotions, all the passions of the great poets.

He may, however, be absorbingly interested and thrilled by "Macbeth," or the "Tempest," or the "Merchant of Venice." He does not get from these plays all that his elders might get, any more than he would perceive the full meaning and passion of a tremendous situation in real life; but he does get some portion of the message, some perception of the deeps and heights of human nature. Even if he find no more than simple, unreasoning enjoyment, he is gaining unconsciously, and he is obviously nourishing a love for good literature.

The question of what is thoroughness in school study of literature is of much importance, and it is of no less difficulty. Certainly it is not merely the mastery of technical obscurities of language, the solving of philological puzzles, or the careful examination of historical facts. Thoroughness in these things, as has already been said, may be exactness in learning about literature, but not in the study of literature itself. Consideration of the average acquirements of pupils in secondary schools makes it fairly evident, it seems to me, that the study of technique in any of its phases cannot in these classes be carried very far without the danger of its degenerating into the most lifeless formalism; and perhaps in nothing else is the tact and judgment of the teacher so well shown as in the decision how far it is wise to carry study along particular lines. I have never encountered a class even in my college work which I could have set to the subjects recommended in a book for teachers of literature which advises drilling the students of the high school on the relations in the plays of Shakespeare "of metre to character," whatever that may mean. Neither should I set them to distinguish, as is advised by another text-book, between "the kinds of imagination employed: (*a*) Modifying; (*b*) Reconstructive; (*c*) Poetical: creative, imperative, or associative." I could not, indeed, do much with such subjects, from the simple fact that I do not myself know what such questions mean, and still less could I answer them. Each instructor, however, must decide for himself, and with every class decide anew. No fixed standard can be established, but each case must be settled on its own merits.

# X

# Examinational

Examinations are at present held to be an essential part of the machinery of education, and whether we do or do not believe this to be true, we are as teachers forced to accept them. Especially is it incumbent on teachers in the secondary schools to pay much attention to accustoming pupils to these ordeals and to preparing them to go through them unscathed. Many instructors, as has been said already, become so completely the slaves to this process that they confine their efforts to it entirely, and few are able to prevent its taking undue importance in their work and in the minds of their pupils.

The general principle should be kept in mind that no examination is of real value for itself in the training of youth, and that to study for it directly and explicitly is fatal to all the higher uses of the study of literature or of anything else. Tests of proficiency and advancement are necessary, but they should be regarded as tests, and no pains should be spared to impress upon every student the fact that beyond this office of measuring attainment they are of no value whatever.

Examinations exist, however, and nothing which can be done directly is likely to remove from the minds of sub-freshmen the notion that they study literature largely if not solely for the sake of being able to struggle successfully with the difficulties of entrance papers. The only means of combating this idea is the indirect method of making the study interesting in and for itself; of nourishing a love for great writings and fostering appreciation of masterpieces. It may be added, moreover, that this is also the surest way of securing ease and proficiency on just those lines in which it is the ambition of pedantic teachers to have their pupils excel. Classes are more effectively trained for college tests by teaching them to think, to examine for themselves, to have real responsiveness and feeling for literature, than they can possibly be by any drill along formal lines. Here as pretty generally in life the indirect is the surest.

More is done in the way of preparation for any rational examination, I believe, by training youth to recognize good literature and to realize what makes it good, than by any amount of deliberate drill of especially prescribed works or laborious following out of the lines indicated by old examination-papers. Much of this is effected by what has been spoken of as inspirational teaching, the simple training of children to have real enjoyment of the best. In the lower grades of school this is all that can be profitably attempted. Before the student leaves the secondary school, however, he should beable for himself to make in a general way an application of the principles which underlie literary distinctions. He should be able broadly to recognize the qualities which belong to the best work. He should be able from personal experience to appreciate the force of the remarks of De Quincey:

> What is it that we mean by literature? Popularly, and amongst the thoughtless, it is held to include everything that is printed in a book. Little logic is required to disturb this definition. The most thoughtless person is easily made aware that in the idea of literature one essential element is some relation to a general and common interest of man, so that what applies only to a local or professional or merely personal interest, even though presenting itself in the shape of a book, will not belong to literature. . . . Men have so little reflected on the higher functions of literature as to find it a paradox if one should describe it as a mean or subordinate purpose of books to give information. But this is a paradox only in the sense

which makes it honorable to be paradoxical. . . . What do you learn from "Paradise Lost"? Nothing at all. What do you learn from a cookery-book? Something new, something you did not know before, in every paragraph. But would you therefore put the wretched cookery-book on a higher level of estimation than the divine poem? What you owe to Milton is not any knowledge, of which a million separate items are still but a million of advancing steps on the same earthly level; what you owe is power, that is, exercise and expansion to your own latent capacity of sympathy with the infinite, where each pulse and each separate influx is a step upward, a step ascending as upon a Jacob's ladder from earth to mysterious altitudes above the earth. All the steps of knowledge, from first to last, carry you further on the same plane, but could never raise you one foot above your ancient level of earth; whereas the very first step in power is a flight, is an ascending movement into another element where earth is forgotten.—"The Poetry of Pope."

If a boy or girl has any vital and personal perception of the truth which is here so eloquently set forth, this perception affords a certain criterion by which to judge whatever work comes to hand. It will also give both the inclination and the power to judge rightly, so that anything which an examination-paper may legitimately ask is in so far within the scope of ordinary thought.

I have ventured, in another chapter, to give some idea of the way in which I think such a work as "Macbeth" might be treated in the secondary school. I wish to emphasize the fact that it is an illustration and not a model. It is the way in which I should do it; but the teaching of literature, I repeat, is naught if it is not marked by the personality of the teacher. Of the results to be aimed at one need not be in doubt; concerning the methods there are and there should be as many opinions as there are sound and individual instructors. This illustration I have included because it may serve as a sort of diagram to make plain things which can only clumsily be presented otherwise, and because I hope that it may be suggestive even to teachers who differ widely from this exact method.

What is aimed at in this manner of treating the play is primarily the enjoyment of the pupil, secondarily the broadening of his mind, and thirdly the training of his powers for the examinations inevitably lying in wait for him. It may seem contradictory that I put pleasure first and yet would begin with straightforward drill on the vocabulary. Such training, however, is preparatory to the taking up of literature, I believe it necessary to the best results, and I have already said that to my mind no need exists for making this dull. Even if it be looked upon as simple drudgery, however, I should not shirk it. Children should be taught that they are to meet hard work pluckily. They cannot evade the multiplication-table without subsequent inconvenience, and the sooner they realize that this is true in principle all through life, the better for them. Their enjoyment, moreover, will be tenfold greater if they earn it by sturdy work.

It would be well, I believe, if all teachers in the secondary schools who are in the habit of concerning themselves largely with examinations and of allowing the minds of those under them to become fixed on these could realize that readers of blue-books are sure to be favorably impressed by two things: by the expression of thoughts obviously individual, and by the evidence of clear thinking. If these two qualities characterize an examination-book, the chances of its passing muster are so large that exact formal knowledge counts for little in comparison. All teachers who are intelligently in earnest try to put as little stress on examinations as is possible under existing conditions, but not all keep clearly in mind the fact that the best remedy for possible harm is the cultivation of the student's individuality.

The question of written work in preparation for entrance tests is a difficult one, and it is one which has been largely answered by the papers set by the colleges. It is natural that teachers who are entirely aware that their own reputations will largely depend upon the success of the candidates they send up should endeavor to train their classes in the especial line of writing which seems best to suit the ideas of examiners. The principle of selection is not, it seems to me, a sound one, but it is inevitable. The one thing which may be done is to make the topics selected as human and as personal as possible: to insist that the boy or girl who is writing of Lady Macbeth or Hamlet shall make the strongest effort possible to realize the character as a real being; shall as far as possible take the attitude of writing concerning some actual person about whom are known the facts set down in the play. This is less difficult than it sounds, and while it is never entirely possible for a child to realize Lady Macbeth as if she were a neighbor, most children can go much farther in this direction than is generally appreciated.

Themes retelling the plot of novel or play are seldom satisfactory. Satisfactorily to summarize the story of a work of any length requires more literary grasp than can possibly be expected in a secondary school. It is far better to set the wits of children to work to fill up gaps of time in the stories as they are originally written; to imagine what Macbeth and his wife had said to each other before he goes to the chamber of Duncan in the second act, for instance, or the talk between Silas Marner and Eppie after the visit in which Godfrey Cass disclosed himself as the girl's father. These are not easy subjects, and it is not to be expected that the grade of work produced will be high, but it is at least likely to be original and genuine.

Description is a snare into which it is easy for teacher or pupil to fall. It generally means the more or less conscious imitation of passages from the reading, or a sort of crazy-quilt of scraps in which sentences of the author are clumsily pieced together. In the highest grades good work may sometimes be obtained by asking pupils to describe the setting of a scene in a play, but this is far too difficult for most classes.

Examination of character, of situations, or of motives affords the best opportunity for written work in connection with literary study.

To make literary study subordinate to the practice of composition is manifestly wrong, yet in many schools this is done in practice even if it is not justified in theory. Children should be taught to write by other means than by themes in connection with the masterpieces of literature. The old cry against using "Paradise Lost," and the soliloquies of Hamlet as exercises in parsing might well be repeated with added emphasis of the modern fashion of making Shakespeare and Milton mere adjuncts to a course in composition. The written work is, of course, to be corrected where it is faulty, but its chief purpose should never be anything outside of the better understanding and appreciation of the authors read.

In a brief, sensible pamphlet on "Methods of Teaching of Novels" May Estelle Cook remarks:

> There is another point which I should like to make for the study of character, though with some hesitation, since there is room for great difference of opinion about it. It is this: that the study of character leads directly to the exercise of the moral instinct. Whether we like it or not, it is true that the school-boy—even the boy, and much more the girl—will raise the question, "Is it right?" and "Is it wrong?" and that we must either answer or ignore these questions. My own feeling about it is that this irrepressible moral instinct was included by Providence partly for the purpose of making a special diversion in favor of the English teacher. . . . A boy will read scenes in "Macbeth" through a dozen times for the sake of deciding whether Macbeth or Lady Macbeth was chiefly responsible for the murder of Duncan, when he will read them only once for the story; and this extra zeal is not so much because he wants to satisfy a craving for facts, as because he enjoys fixing praise or blame. . . . My experience with the Sir Roger de Coverley papers has been that the class failed to get any imaginative grasp of them until I frankly appealed to the moral instinct

by asking, "What did Addison mean to teach in this paper?" "Did the Eighteenth Century need that lesson?" and "Do we still need it?" By that process the class have finally reached a grasp of Sir Roger which has given them fortitude to write a theme on "Sir Roger at an Afternoon Tea."

My own definition of imagination is evidently not that of the writer, and I am not able to agree that this appeal to the moral instinct develops anything other than an intellectual understanding; but that point is unimportant here. The thing which is to be noted is that on the moral side children may be able to think intelligently and individually in regard to the characters and the situations of the plays and the novels read. The teacher, in choosing such subjects for written work, must, of course, be careful to avoid topics which have already been considered in the book itself. In a novel by George Eliot, for instance, all possible moral issues are likely to be so discussed and rediscussed by the novelist as to leave little room for the thought of the reader to exercise itself independently; but in all the plays of Shakespeare, and in the fiction of most of the masters, the opportunities are ample.

The supreme test of any subject which is to be given to students in their written work is whether it is one upon which it is reasonable to suppose they can and will have thought which is individual and therefore original. If it were necessary to make nice distinctions between that which is and that which is not legitimately part of the study of literature as an art, one must go much further than this. The writing of themes, however, is part of the examinational side of the work; the main thing is to be sure that it is not dwelt upon more than is necessary, and that it is within the range of the personal experience of the student. If teachers feel compelled to set their classes to write formal and lifeless themes on pedantic topics such as too often appear in examination-papers, they will do well to keep in mind that this is not the study of literature, but a stultifying process which lessens the power of appreciation and replaces intelligent comprehension by mechanical imitation.

In connection with the subject of this chapter I may mention a device which may not be without practical value in secondary-school examinations. It affords a means of discovering how well the student is succeeding in grasping general principles and in making actual application of them; while at the same time it should impress upon him the fact that he is not studying merely a series of required readings, but the nature and qualities of literature.

On an examination-paper in second-year English at the Institute of Technology was put this test:

> It is assumed that the student has never read the following extract. State what seem its excellent points (*a*) of workmanship; (*b*) of thought; (*c*) of imagination.

To this was added a brief extract from some standard author.

The opening statement was made in order that the class should understand the selection to be not from any required reading, but from some work presumably entirely unfamiliar. The points of excellence only were asked for in order to fix attention on merits; and indirectly to strengthen, so far as might be, the perception of the importance of looking in literature for merits rather than for defects. It is undoubtedly proper that scholars should be able to perceive defects, but this power is best trained by educating them to be sensitive and responsive to excellencies.[8]

The necessities of time made it impossible to put upon the papers of which I am speaking extracts of much length, and the class were told that not much was expected in comment upon the thought expressed. The purpose of the question, that of seeing how intelligently they were able to apply such principles as they had learned, was also

---

8   See page 205.

frankly put. They were warned against generalities and statements unsupported. Then they were left to their own devices. The results were all suggestive, and of course were of widely varying degrees of merit. A few samples may be given, chosen, I confess, from those more interesting. On one paper were the opening lines of the second book of "Paradise Lost."

> High on a throne of royal state, which far
> Outshone the wealth of Ormus and of Ind,
> Or where the gorgeous east with richest hand
> Showers on her kings barbaric pearl and gold,
> Satan exalted sat.

Among the comments were these:

Of the workmanship of this selection we may say that it is good. The selection of words is especially forcible. "Gorgeous east" and "richest hand" are extremely so. But what I consider a fine use of a word is the word "barbaric." Here we can see the early inhabitants of the uncivilized rich countries of the east; the inhabitants ignorant of the value of their wealth, throwing it around as we would the pebbles on a beach. The thought and the imagination are good. We can see before us the vividly portrayed picture. There sits Satan high above his surrounding in such rich and dazzling magnificence that it outshines even the richest kings of the richest part of the world.

The best point of the workmanship consists in placing the description first and not completing the thought until the last line; thus keeping the reader in suspense, and causing careful attention to be put on all the sentence. The words "high," "throne," "royal," and "exalted" combine to bring out the thought of Satan's majesty. The thought of unbounded wealth is brought out by the use of the word "showers" in the third line. The author is able to give us a much more vivid idea of the magnificence of the throne by letting us construct the throne to suit ourselves than by giving a detailed description and leaving nothing to the imagination. Even the materials are only suggested, the whole idea being one of unbounded wealth and splendor.

The choice of words is one of the best points in the workmanship of the quotation. The arrangement also adds emphasis. All the descriptions of the throne are so vivid that the mind is deeply impressed by the splendor and richness of the throne. The "gorgeous east" is very expressive of wealth and beauty. With this arrangement of words the piece becomes very striking and the choice of the strongest words is shown too in touch with the whole sentence. Whereas on the other hand if any other arrangement had been used much of the force of these words would have been lost. The thought of the extract is to describe the great wealth and beauty with which Satan is surrounded. The writer must have a very vivid imagination to describe such a scene of wealth and beauty. The first word, "High," appeals directly to the imagination and immediately gives the impression of power.

These answers were written by boys who had not been called upon to do anything of the sort before, and while their inadequacy is evident enough, they are genuine, and are sound as far as they go. Of course, after such a test, the first business of the teacher is to go over the selection and to show how he would himself have answered the question. The class is then ready to appreciate qualities which might be recited to them in vain before they have set their minds to the problem. In the examples I have given no one has touched, for instance, upon the suggestiveness of the words "Ormus" and "Ind," but very little is needed to make them see this after they have had the passage in an examination-paper.

A couple of examples dealing with the first two stanzas of Byron's "Destruction of Sennacherib" may be given by way of showing how a different selection was treated.

The first thing I noticed in reading the extract was the perfect rhythm. You cannot read the extract without wanting to say it aloud. Then the choice of words struck me: "The *sheen* of their spears;" "when summer is *green*." It is hard for me to distinguish workmanship, thought, and imagination. I cannot tell whether the words and metaphors used in the extract were the result of deliberate choice and of long thought; but I strongly suspect that he saw the whole thing in his imagination, and the words just came to him. It is hard to understand how anything that reads so smoothly could have been written with labor. The strongest point of the extract seems to be its richness in illustration: "The Assyrian came down like the wolf on the fold." No long, detailed description could explain better the wildness of such an attack, the sudden swoop of some half-barbaric horde, striking suddenly, and then disappearing into the night. "The sheen of the spears was like stars on the sea." The flash from a spear would be just such a gleam as the reflected star from the crest of a wave, visible for a moment and then gone.

Some of its excellent points of workmanship are melody and selection of words. The melody is excellent. It has a soothing effect when read aloud, and there is not a place where one would hesitate in regard to the accenting of words. I believe the melody is so good that a person only knowing the pronunciation of the first line could almost read the rest of it correctly because the sound of each line is so closely connected with that of all other lines. The selection of words is very good. There is not a place where a substitution could be made which would improve the meaning, sense, or melody. The extract shows great thought. In the last paragraph especially where the Assyrians are compared to the leaves of summer and in autumn. No better thought could bring out more clearly how badly the host was defeated. In the first paragraph it also compares the Assyrians to a wolf coming down upon a fold. This again gives a definite idea, and seems to point out how confident they were of victory. The imagination is very vivid. You can almost think you were on the field and that all the events were taking place before you.

I have copied these partly to emphasize the point that it is idle to expect too much, and partly to illustrate the form in which genuine perception is likely to work out upon a school examination-paper. These have not been chosen as the best papers written, but each is good because each shows sincere opinion.

This sort of question is of course in the line of what is constantly done in class, but it is after all a different thing when it is made to emphasize the idea that an examination is a test of the power to appreciate literature instead of an exercise of memory.

# XI

# The Study of Prose

Method in teaching is properly the adaptation of the personality of a given teacher to the personality of a given class. It cannot be defined by hard and fast rules, and the only value in presenting such illustrations as the following is that they may afford hints which teachers will be able with advantage to develop in terms of their own individuality. The way that is wise in one is never to be set down as the way best for another; and here as elsewhere I offer not a model but simply an illustration. If it suggest, it has fulfilled a better purpose than if it were taken blindly as a rigid guide.

My own feeling would be that classes in literature should be provided with nothing but the bare text, without notes of any kind unless with a glossary of terms not to be found in available books of reference. In the matter of looking up difficulties the books of reference in the school library should be used; and if the school has no library beyond the dictionary, I should still hold to my opinion. The vocabulary may be very largely worked out with any fairly comprehensive dictionary, and what cannot be discovered in this way is better taken *viva voce* in recitation than swallowed from notes without even the trouble of asking. Much will be done, moreover, by the not unhealthy spirit of emulation which is sure to exist where the pupils are set to use their wits and to report the result in class. They will remember much better; and, what in general education is of the very first importance, they will have admirable practice in the use of books of reference. Many difficulties must be explained by the teacher; but this, I insist, is better than the following of notes, a habit which is sure to degenerate into lifeless memorizing. The model text for school use would be cut in those few passages not suited for the school-room, would be clearly printed, and would be as free as possible from any outside matter whatever. In the case of poetry the ideal method would be to keep the text out of the hands of the student altogether until all work necessary to the mastering of the vocabulary had been done: but in practice such voluntary reading as a pupil chose to do beforehand would do no harm other than possibly to distract his attention from the learning of the meaning of words and phrases. In prose he will generally be in a key which allows the interruption of a pause for looking up words without much injury to the effect of the work.

The study of prose is of course directed by the same principles as that of poetry, but the application is in school-work somewhat modified in details. In the first place the vocabulary of any prose used in the schools is not likely to contain obsolete words such as are found in Shakespeare, and in the second place the length of a novel forbids its being read aloud in class in its entirety. I have taken my illustrations chiefly from books included in the College Requirements, because these books are the ones with which the majority of teachers are obliged to work. The Sir Roger de Coverley papers are sure to be taken up in any school-room where literature is studied to-day, and Burke "On Conciliation" is one of the inevitable obstacles in the way of every boy who wishes to enter college. Whatever the work, however, the important thing is that each pupil shall understand, shall appreciate, and shall connect what he reads with his own life.

The order in which different works are taken up in class is a matter of much moment. No rules can be given arbitrarily to govern the arrangement of the readings, since much depends upon the individual class to be dealt with. On general principles, for instance, it might seem that Burke's "Speech," as being the least imaginative of the prescribed work, might well come first; but on the other hand, the argument demands intellectual capacity and maturity which will often require that it be not put before a given group of scholars until they have had all the training they can gain from the other requirements. A teacher can hardly afford to have any rule in the whole treatment of literature which is not so flexible that it may be modified or disregarded entirely when circumstances require. The ideal method, perhaps, would be to give a class first a few short pieces as tests, and then to arrange their longer work upon the basis of the result.

If the "Speech" is to be taken up first or last, it must be preceded by a clear understanding of the history of the conditions with which Burke dealt. This knowledge should have been obtained in the history class, and the use of facts obtained in another branch affords one of the opportunities for doing that useful thing which should be kept always in sight, the enforcing of the fact that all education is one, although for convenience of handling necessarily divided into various branches. If the class has not had the requisite instruction in history, the teacher of English is forced to pause and supply the deficiency, as it is hopeless to try to go on without it. The argument of Burke is pretty tough work for any class of high-school students, and without familiarity with the circumstances which called it forth is utterly unintelligible.

The vocabulary of Burke contains few words which need to be studied beforehand, and indeed it is perhaps better to treat the speech as so far a logical rather than an imaginative work that without other preparation than a thorough mastery of the circumstances under which it was delivered and of the political issues with which it dealt the class may be given the text directly. In the first reading the thing to be insured is the intelligent comprehension of the language and of the argument. In the first half-dozen paragraphs, for instance, such passages as these must be made perfectly clear:

> I hope, Sir, that notwithstanding the austerity of the Chair, your good nature will incline you to some degree of indulgence toward human frailty.

The grand penal bill.

Returned to us from the other House.

We are not at all embarrassed (unless we please to make ourselves so) by any incongruous mixture of coercion and restraint.

From being blown about by every wind of fashionable doctrine.

This is clear enough in meaning, but the class should notice the suggestion of the biblical phrase which insinuates that a good deal of the political fluctuation which has complicated the question of the treatment of the colonies has been like the hysterical instability of those who run after every fresh eccentricity offered in the name of religion.

I really did not think it safe or manly to have fresh principles to seek upon every fresh mail that should arrive from America.

It is in your equity to judge.

Parliament, having an enlarged view of objects.

A situation which I will not miscall, which I dare not name.

That the public tribunal (never too indulgent to a long and unsuccessful opposition) would now scrutinize our conduct with unusual severity.

We must produce our hand.

Somewhat disreputably.

The whole oration is studded with passages such as these, and it is the habit of too many instructors to expect the student to depend upon notes for the solution of such difficulties. I have already indicated that I believe this to be an unwise and weakening process; and in a political document of this sort a drill for elucidating difficulties may well be undertaken when in an imaginative work more latitude may be allowed in the way of sliding over them.

The reading of the speech as a whole could hardly be attempted with any profit until the class has mastered its technicalities and its logic. The oration differs in this from more imaginative literature. Here it is not only proper but necessary to make analysis part of the first reading.

The class should for itself make a summary of the speech as it goes forward. For each paragraph should be devised a single sentence which gives clearly and concisely the thought, so that at the conclusion a complete skeleton shall have been made. Each student should make these sentences for himself as part of his preparation of a lesson, and from a comparison in the class the final form may be selected. Some of the school editions do this admirably, but one of two things seems to me indisputable: either the "Speech" is too difficult for students to handle or they should make their own summaries. To do this part of the work for them is to deprive the study of its most valuable element. The best justification such a selection can have for its inclusion in the list of required books is that it may fairly be used for this careful analytical work without prejudice to the effect of the piece as a whole. In other words, no objection exists to treating this especial selection first from the purely intellectual point of view. To consider a play of Shakespeare first intellectually would seem to me utterly wrong; but this argument of Burke is intentionally addressed to the reason rather than to the imagination, and would therefore logically be so read.

Beside the mere interpretation of difficult passages, the pupil should be made to discern and to weigh the value and effect of the admirable sentences in which the orator has condensed whole trains of logic.

The concessions of the weak are the concessions of fear.

A wise and salutary neglect.

The power of refusal, the first of all revenues.

The voluntary flow of heaped-up plenty.

All government—indeed, every human benefit and enjoyment, every virtue and every prudent act—is founded on compromise and barter.

The study of phrases of this sort is admirable training for the reasoning faculties of the scholar, it educates the powers of reading, and it may be made a continuous lesson in the nature and value of literary technique. Of this study of literary workmanship I shall speak later; here it is sufficient to point the necessity at once and the advantage of dwelling on these vital thoughts so admirably expressed.

By the time the oration has been gone through with, and a summary of each paragraph made in the class, a skeleton is ready from which the argument may be considered as a whole. In some schools students will be able to criticise from an historical point of view, and any intelligent boy to whom the oration is given for study should be able to judge of the logic of the plea.

If the "Speech" is to justify its claim to being literature in the higher sense, however, it is not possible to stop with the intellectual study. The question of what constitutes literature is better taken up, it seems to me, near the end of the course of secondary work, if it is to come in at all; but preparation for dealing with that question must come all along the line. When Burke has been studied for his political meanings, his argument summed up and examined, the intellectual force of the parts and of the whole sufficiently considered, then it is necessary to look at the imaginative qualities of the work.

I would never set children to examine any piece of prose or verse for any qualities until I was sure they understood what they are to look for. If they are to examine the oration for imaginative passages, they must first know clearly what an imaginative passage is. Here the previous training of the class is to be reckoned with. Some classes must be taught the significance of the term "imaginative" by having the passages pointed out to them and then analyzed; others are so far advanced as to be able to discover them. The thing I wish to emphasize is that when the simply intellectual study has progressed far enough, the imaginative must follow. Passages which may be used here are such as these:

> My plan . . . does not propose to fill your lobby with squabbling colony agents, who will require the interposition of your mace at every instant to keep peace among them. It does not institute a magnificent auction of finance, where captivated provinces come to general ransom by bidding against each other, until you knock down the hammer, and determine a proportion of payments beyond all powers of algebra to equalize and settle.

> Such is the strength with which population shoots in that part of the world, that, state the numbers as high as we will, whilst the dispute continues, the exaggeration ends.

> Look at the manner in which the people of New England have of late carried on the whale fishery. Whilst we follow them among the tumbling mountains of ice, and behold them penetrating into the deepest frozen recesses of Hudson Bay and Davis Strait, whilst we are looking for them beneath the Arctic Circle, we hear that they have pierced into the opposite region of polar cold, that they are at the antipodes and engaged under the frozen Serpent of the south. Falkland Island, which seemed too remote and romantic an object for the grasp of national ambition, is but a stage and resting-place in the progress of their victorious industry. Nor is the equinoctial heat more discouraging to them than the accumulated winter of both poles. We know that while some of them draw the line and strike the harpoon on the coast of Africa, others run the longitude and pursue their gigantic game along the coast of Brazil. No sea but is vexed by their fisheries. No climate that is not witness of their toils.

> A people who are still, as it were, but in the gristle, and not yet hardened into the bone of manhood.

Passages of this sort are frequent in the speech, and it is not difficult to make the pupils not only recognize them, but appreciate the quality which distinguishes them from the matter-of-fact statements of figures, statistics, or other necessary information.

A step further is to make the class see how the imagination shows in a passage like the famous sentence:

> I do not know the method of drawing up an indictment against a whole people.

These dozen or so words may profitably be made the subject for an entire lesson, and if this seem a proportionately extravagant amount of time to give to a single line, I can only say that to do one thing thoroughly is not only better than to do a score superficially, but in the long run it is economy of time as well. If the class can be led to discuss the meaning of the phrase, and the principles upon which Burke rested the argument which is behind this superb proposition, not only will the hour have been well spent in developing the ideas of the students, but the whole oration will be wonderfully illuminated. When to this is added an adequate understanding of the imaginative grasp which seizes the personality of a whole nation, perceives its majesty, its sovereignty, and the impossibility of arraigning it before the bar like a criminal, the student is getting the best that the study of the oration can give him.

Written work should be kept within the limits of the capability of the individual pupil to think intelligently. Perhaps the best means of enforcing upon a class the vigor of Burke's style at once and the completeness of the oration as a whole is that of requiring from each an expression, as clear and as exact as possible, of just what the orator wished to effect, and an estimate, as critical as the pupil is capable of making, of how the means employed were especially adapted to carry out his purpose. Such work will be useless if the teacher does the reasoning, but much may be elicited by skilful leading in recitation, and after the scholars have done all that they can do, the instructor may add his comment.

After the "Speech on Conciliation" may reasonably come, if the required list of readings is being followed, the "Sir Roger de Coverley Papers." Here one deals with work more deliberately imaginative. Preparation for taking up these essays should begin with a brief account of the "Spectator" and of the circumstances under which they were written. The less elaborate this is the better, so long as it serves the purpose of giving the class some notion of the point of view; and indeed it is to be doubted whether as a matter of fact any great harm would be done if even this were omitted. What is needed is to interest the class in the work, and facts about times and circumstances seldom effect much real good in this study.

The vocabulary will give little trouble. It is well to be sure that the readers understand beforehand such words as may be rather remote from daily speech. In the account of the club (March 2, 1710-11), for instance, the list given out for test might include such terms as these: baronet, country-dance, shire, humor, modes, Soho-square, quarter-sessions, game-act. In the first paragraph, from which these words are taken, are also two or three phrases which should be familiar before the reading is undertaken: "never dressed afterward," "in his merry humors," "rather beloved than esteemed," and "justice of the quorum." The historical allusions, as represented by the names Lord Rochester, Sir George Etherege, and Dawson, go also into this preliminary study.

The paper should be first read as a whole, with no other interruption than may come in the form of questions from the class. The teacher should make no effort at anything here but intelligent reading. Then the paper may be given out for careful study; the form of this may be varied at the pleasure of the teacher and the needs of the class. The presentation of character is the point to be most strongly brought out, and this must be done delicately but as completely as possible. The "De Coverley Papers" necessarily seem to the modern youth extremely remote from actual life as he knows it, and the majority of Institute students with whom I have talked admit that they found Addison very quiet, or, in their own phrase, "slow." The characters are accordingly apt to appear to them dim and unreal; to be hardly more alive than the figures on an ancient tapestry. This feeling cannot be wholly overcome, especially in the limited time which is at the command of the teacher of school literature, yet whatever vividness of impression a reader of the essays gets is directly proportional to the extent to which Sir Roger and his friends emerge from the land of shadows, and seem to the boys and girls genuine flesh and blood. The chief care of the instructor in dealing with these papers, the aim to which everything else should be subordinated, is to encourage and to develop the sense of reality. The little touches by which the personality of the old knight is shown must be dwelt upon as each appears; and in the end a summary of these may be made as a means of stating briefly but clearly Sir Roger's character. Constantly, too, by means homely enough to be clearly and easily intelligible to the class, must each of these passages be connected with the personal experiences of the children. In the essay generally headed "Sir Roger at Home," for instance, the author remarks:

> Sir Roger, who is very well acquainted with my humor, lets me rise and go to bed when I please; dine at his own table, or in my chamber, as I think fit; sit still, and say nothing, without bidding me be merry.

The whole situation, that of a notable man's visit to a country squire, is utterly foreign to the pupil's probable experience. He can, however, be made to recall occasions in which he has been considered and his wishes consulted. He may or may not as a guest have tested different forms of hospitality, but he easily decides how under given circumstances he would wish to be treated. From this he is without difficulty led to an appreciation of the consideration with which Sir Roger was intent not upon his own wishes or the ease of his household, but upon the pleasure of his guest. Few boys or girls can have come to the school age without understanding what a drawback to good spirits it is to be told to be merry, and they can appreciate the common sense of the knight in thinking of this, and his tact in not bothering his guest. The same thoughtful kindness is shown in the way Sir Roger protected his lion from sightseers. Incidentally the point may be made in passing that Addison humorously took this means of impressing on the reader of the "Spectator" the importance of the supposed writer.

The best preparation a teacher can make for dealing with these essays is to get clearly into his own mind the personality, the characteristics, even the outward appearance of each of the characters dealt with. It is impossible to make these quiet and delicately drawn pictures real and alive unless we have for them a genuine love and a sense of acquaintance; and I know of no method by which in practical work this can be communicated except by the vivifying of such passages as that quoted above.

Each student should bring to the class a statement of what he regards as the chief thought in each paper as it comes up,—not the moral of the paper, but the chief end which the writer seems to have in view, the thought which most strongly strikes the reader. These opinions should be talked over in class, and from them one produced which at least the majority of the class are willing to accept. No pupil, however, should be discouraged from holding to his own original proposition, or from adopting a view at variance with that of the majority.

Always if possible,—and personally I should make it possible, even at the sacrifice of other things,—the paper should last of all be read as a whole without interruption. The fact should always be kept before the minds of the pupils that the essay is not a collection of detached facts or thoughts, but that it is a whole, and that it can fairly be received only in its entirety.

To stretch out illustrations of the teaching of particular books would only be tedious, and I trust I have done enough to make evident what I believe should be the spirit of work done in the "studying" of prose in the secondary schools. The matter is of comparative simplicity as contrasted with the handling of poetry; and I have therefore reserved most of my space for the latter. No one knows better than I that any formal method is fatal to real and vital work; and what I have written has been largely inspired by a knowledge that many instructors are at a loss to formulate any rational method at all, while others, I am forced sorrowfully to add, seem never even to have perceived that any method is possible.

# XII

# The Study of the Novel

Whatever may be the entrance requirements and whatever the prescribed course in the way of fiction, I should begin the study of the novel with a modern book. To hold the attention of the majority of modern children long enough for them to form any adequate idea of the quality and characteristics of any work of the length of an ordinary novel, long enough for them to gain an idea which conceives of the work as a whole and not as a collection of detached scenes and scraps, is sufficiently difficult in any case. It should not be made more difficult by selecting as a text a book requiring effort in the understanding of vocabulary, point of view, setting, and the rest. "Ivanhoe" is good in its place, but it is not adapted to use as first aid to the untrained. It is probable that a class after sufficient experience in fiction may be able to handle "Silas Marner," and it is apparently fated by the powers that be that they must struggle with "The Vicar of Wakefield;" but they certainly need preliminary practice before they are set to grapple with those fictions so remote from their daily lives. They should begin with something as near their own world as possible; and "Treasure Island," the scene laid in the land of boyhood's imaginings, is an excellent example of the sort of story which may well be used to introduce them to the serious consideration of this branch of literature.

A little preliminary talk may well precede the actual reading. The teacher should be sure that the class has a fair idea of what piracy is,—a matter generally of little difficulty,—and of the social conditions under which the tale begins. The actual geography of the romance need not be considered much, although students lose nothing if they are trained to the habit of knowing accurately the location of such real places as are named in any story; but the imaginary geography of the tale, the topography of the island, should be well mastered. Beyond this, the teacher should have prepared a list of words to be learned before any reading is done. This should include all those in the first assignment that are likely to bother the child in the first going over of the text. In the opening chapter, for instance, such words as these:

- Buccaneer (title of Part I).
- Capstan bars.
- Connoisseur.
- Dry Tortugas.
- Spanish Main.
- Hawker.
- Assizes.

In this chapter are a couple of allusions to the costume of the time, but as they are intelligible only when taken as sentences they may be left for the reading in class:

One of the cocks of his hat having fallen down.

The neat, bright doctor, with his powder as white as snow.

When the class comes together the vocabulary is to be taken up as a solid and distinct task, and after that is disposed of, the text may follow. It is generally impossible to give the time to the reading aloud of an entire novel; but I am inclined to believe that at least the opening chapters, the portion of the story which must be most deliberately considered if the young reader is to go on with the tale in full possession of the atmosphere and the characters as they are introduced, should always be thus taken up. The portions assigned for each lesson must be brief at first, but may wisely increase as the interest grows and familiarity with personages and situations is enlarged.

The first chapter, then, having been read aloud, the class may make a list of the characters introduced: Squire Trelawney, Dr. Livesey, the old pirate not yet named, the father, the "I" who is telling the story. The seaman who brings the chest and the neighbors are obviously of no permanent importance.

Of these characters the class should give orally so much of an impression as they have obtained from this chapter. This is simple with the buccaneer, fairly easy in regard to Dr. Livesey and the inn-keeper, but more difficult in the case of the boy. The paragraph beginning:

How that personage haunted my dreams, I need scarcely tell you—

and the opening sentence of the following paragraph:

But though I was so terrified by the idea of the seafaring man with one leg, I was far less afraid of the captain himself than anybody else who knew him—

give admirable material for class discussion. The first should appeal to the children, who must be made to understand that to Jim Hawkins the one-legged seafaring man was not a mere idea, but an actual personage for whom he was set to watch, and of whom even the terrible old Billy Bones was mortally afraid. The second at once illustrates how the unknown was more frightful to the lad than the veritable flesh and blood pirate; and it shows also by excellent contrast how terrifying the buccaneer was to the frequenters of the inn.

For the second chapter the vocabulary would for most classes include such words as

- Cutlass.
- Talons.

- Chine.

- Lancet.

The expressions which should be made clear in class would include:

- Cleared the hilt of his cutlass.

- Showed a wonderfully clean pair of heels.

- Fouled the tap.

- Stake my wig.

- Open a vein.

This chapter has a number of delicate touches which should be brought to the notice of the class; such as the lump in the throat of Black Dog while he waited for the pirate in moral terror; his clever excuse for having the door left open apparently that he might be sure Jim was not listening, but in reality that he might have a way of escape in case of danger; the picture of the gallows in the tattooing.

The characters of Billy Bones and Jim are added to in the chapter, and that of the doctor made more clear. The touch by which the boy is made to feel compassion for the pirate when Bones turns so ghastly at the sight of Black Dog is one which should not be missed. The story, too, begins to develop, and the youthful reader must be unusually insensitive if he does not speculate upon the past of Bones and upon the relation of the pirate with Black Dog.

It is not necessary to go on with this sort of analysis, for the method I am detailing must be essentially that of most teachers. If the points mentioned seem to some over-minute, I can only say that since the aim is to teach children how to handle fiction, the task of training them to be intelligently careful in their reading is of the first importance. There is no risk of making them finical or too minutely observant. This is moreover the *study* of a novel, and it should be more careful than reading is supposed to be. It is morally certain that any child will fall below the standard set, and it is therefore necessary to have the standard as high as it can be without tiring or confusing the children.

When the book has been gone through in this way comes the important question of dealing with it as a whole. It would hardly be wise to ask children directly what they think of a book as a complete work; and yet that is the thing at which the teacher wishes to arrive. The way has been prepared by the study of character and the discussion of incident throughout. In the end the subject of character as it is seen from the beginning of the tale to the close may easily lead the way to making up some estimate of the book as a unit. First, do the persons in the romance act consistently; second, do the incidents follow along so that they seem really to have happened. These questions will at first have a tendency to bewilder young readers, who are likely to accept anything in a romance as if it were true, and to have no judgment beyond the matter whether the book does or does not interest them. It is not to be expected that they will go very deep or be very broad in their dealing with such points in the case of a first novel, but they can make a beginning. They cannot in the book in question go far in what is the natural third question concerning a book as a whole: Does it show clearly and truly the development of character under the circumstances of the story. Jim Hawkins is at the end of the book manifestly older and more manly than at the start, as shown, for instance, by his refusal to break his word to Silver when the doctor talks with him over the stockade and urges him to come away with him. With the other characters it is more the bringing out of traits already existing than the developing of new ones. John Silver is of course by far the most masterly figure in the book—although the student should be allowed to have his own idea in regard to this. Indeed, one of the ways in which he judges and should judge a book as a whole is by deciding what personage in it is, all things considered and the story taken all through, most clearly and sharply defined. The class should be able to see and to appreciate how the tale as it progresses brings to light one phase after another of the amazing character of Silver, up to his pluck at the moment when the treasure-seekers discover that the gold has been taken away from the cache and to his humble attitude toward the Squire when the cave of Ben Gunn is reached.

Lastly, perhaps,—for I do not insist upon the order in which these points should be taken up, but only give them in the sequence which to me seems likely to be most natural and effective,—the class should be brought to appreciate the construction of the book. This involves obviously the way in which the author weaves together incidents so that each shall have a part in the general scheme; but it also involves the way in which he brings out the part that the individual traits and character of the persons in the story had in leading up to the end. In "Treasure Island," for instance, it is easy to show how one thing leads to another, and how out of the chain no link could be taken without breaking the continuity. This should not be impressed upon the class, however, as a matter of invention on the part of the author. Children know that the book is a fiction, but they prefer to ignore this. It is not well to make the fact part of the instruction. The way to handle this is to dwell upon the skill with which he has arranged particulars, and passed in his narrative from one party to another so as to have each incident clear. Pupils may be reminded of how easy it is to mix the details of a story so as to confuse the hearer or the reader, and thus may be made to appreciate to some degree the cleverness of the workmanship which so distinguishes the work of Stevenson.

More subtle in a way and yet not beyond the comprehension of the school-boy is the part which character plays in shaping events and moulding the story. The restlessness and the curiosity of Jim, from the adventure of the apple-barrel to the saving of the ship, are essentials in the tale; and equally the diabolical cleverness and *unscrupulousness* of Silver shape the events of the story from beginning to end.

One more illustration may be taken from the novel which is so generally included in high-school English, Scott's "Ivanhoe." Here it is necessary to prepare for the story by the acquirement of a certain amount of history. It is perhaps as well to take the first five[9] paragraphs of the opening chapter as a preliminary lesson, and to treat it as history pure and simple. In preparation for this lesson the following vocabulary should be mastered:

- Dragon of Wantley.

- Wars of the Roses.

- Vassalage.

- Inferior gentry, or franklins.

- Feudal.

- The Conquest.

- Duke William of Normandy.

- Normans.

- Anglo-Saxons.

- Battle of Hastings.

- Laws of the chase.

- Chivalry.

- Hinds.

- Classical languages.

A few other expressions, such as "petty kings," should be looked after in the reading, lest the class get a false impression. The geography of the river Don and of Doncaster may be passed over; but it is perhaps better, especially in this historical preliminary, to require full accuracy in this particular. To my thinking all this should be looked up by the students, and never taken from notes appended to the text.

---

9   Five in the original. Some school editions, for what reason I do not know, omit paragraph five, which begins: "This state of things I have thought it necessary to premise."

The five paragraphs in which Scott gives the historic background should be taken frankly as a piece of work out of which the class is to make as clear a conception of the period of the tale as possible. The pupils should use their common sense and their intelligence in studying it, getting all out of it that they can get. Then it should be read aloud in the class, and carefully gone over. The aim should be to have understood as clearly as possible what were the political and the social conditions of the time when the events of the romance are represented as taking place. Such other historic personages as enter into the story without being mentioned in this preliminary sketch should be brought into this exposition. Thus when King Richard and Prince John and Robin Hood the semi-historic come upon the stage the student will be prepared for the effect which the novelist intended, and will have, moreover, that pleasure which a young reader always feels in finding himself equal to an occasion.

This preliminary work being accomplished, the rest of the book will probably have to be largely assigned for home reading. The opening chapters, however, and the most striking scenes must certainly be read aloud in class. A sufficient portion for a lesson will be assigned each day. A list of words for that portion will be given out with it to be learned first. No teacher will suppose, I fancy, that in every case a student will master the vocabulary before he reads the selection, but the principle is sound and the words would at least be all taken up in class before any reading is done. Students should be told to read the selection aloud at home, and should come to the class acquainted with the meaning and significance of each passage, or prepared to ask about them.

At the beginning of the novel, when the reader is learning the situation and the characters concerned, the assignments must be shorter than in the latter part of the book, when these things are understood and the current of the tale runs more swiftly. The remainder of the first chapter, from the paragraph beginning "The sun was setting" is quite enough for a first instalment. The following words make up the preliminary vocabulary:

- Rites of druidical superstition.
- Scrip.
- Bandeau.
- Harlequin.
- Rational.
- Quarter-staff.
- Murrain.
- Eumæus.

The method of treating the fiction itself has been sufficiently indicated in the previous illustration from "Treasure Island," but may be briefly touched upon. In this chapter of "Ivanhoe" are introduced two characters. Both are described at some length, but in the case of both important touches here and there add to the impression. Gurth is said at the beginning to be stern and sad, and in the talk the reasons come out.

"The mother of mischief confound the Ranger of the forest, that cuts the foreclaws off our dogs, and makes them unfit for their trade."

"Little is left us but the air we breathe, and that appears to have been reserved with much hesitation, solely for the purpose of enabling us to endure the tasks they lay upon our shoulders."

We have a proof of his impulsiveness in the dangerous freedom with which he speaks to Wamba, and of how daring this is we are made aware when the jester says to him:

"I know thou thinkest me a fool, or thou wouldst not be so rash in putting thy head into my mouth. One word to Reginald Front-de-Bœuf . . . thou wouldst waver on one of these trees as a terror to all evil speakers against dignities."

Of the superstition of Gurth we have proof by his fear at the mention of the fairies.

"Wilt thou talk of such things while a terrible storm of thunder and lightning is raging within a few miles of us?"

Here is a fairly satisfactory portrait of Gurth, although other traits of character are developed as the book goes forward. At the end of the novel the attention of the class may be directed to the skilful way in which at the very start Scott has struck in the words of Gurth the keynote of the oppression of the Normans and the hatred for them in the hearts of the Saxons; but a point of this sort should not be anticipated. It will tell for more if it is left until it has had its full effect and its place as a part of the whole romance may be clearly shown.

One last word I cannot bring myself to omit. I have said elsewhere that I disbelieve in the drawing of morals, and at the risk of repetition I wish to emphasize this in connection with fiction. The temptation here is especially strong. It is so easy to draw a moral from any tale ever written that two classes of teachers, those morally over-conscientious and those ignorantly inept, are almost sure to insist that their classes shall drag a moral lesson out of every story. The habit seems to me thoroughly vicious. It is proper to make the character of the persons in the novel as vivid as possible. The villain may be made as hateful to God and to man as the testimony of the author will in any way allow; but when that is done the children should be left to draw their own morals. They should not even be allowed to know that the teacher is aware that a moral may be drawn, and still less should they be asked to discover one. If they draw a moral themselves or ask questions about one, this is well, so long as they are sincere and spontaneous. If they are left entirely to themselves in this they will in a healthy natural fashion get from the story such moral instruction as they are capable of profiting by, and they will not be put into that antagonistic attitude which human nature inevitably takes when it is preached to.

# XIII

# The Study of "Macbeth"

How I conceive the study of poetry may be managed in school-work I have already indicated somewhat fully, but one concrete example is often worth a dozen abstract statements. In the literary work of almost every high school is now included the study of at least one Shakespearean play, and as "Macbeth" is so generally selected as the one to be first taken up, I have chosen that as an illustration.

The study of any play, as I have said, should begin with a requirement that the class master the vocabulary. The pupils should be made to understand that the need of doing this is precisely the same as the need of learning common speech for the sake of comprehending the talk of every-day life, or of mastering the vocabulary of French before going to the theatre to hear a play in that language. The scholars should be told frankly that this will not be particularly easy work, but that it is to be taken in the same spirit that one learned the multiplication-table. No harm can come of letting the class expect this part of the work to be full harder than it really is, and at least it is well to have students understand that they are expected to labor to fit themselves for the enjoyment of literature.

In this preparation the aim is to make it possible for the readers to go on with the text without important interruptions. This purpose determines what words and passages shall be taken up. Some difficulties may safely and wisely be left for the second reading of the play, and as it is well in these days not to expect too much of the industry of youth, the teacher will do well to keep the list of words to be mastered as short as may be. The whole play should be prepared for before any of it is read, but I give only examples from the first act. I should suggest—each teacher to vary the list at his pleasure— that in the first act the following words should be dealt with. The numbers of the lines are those of the Temple Edition.

*Alarum.* This occurs in the stage-directions of scene ii. The class will see at once that it differs from "alarm," and can be made to appreciate how from the strong rolling of the *r*—"alarr'm" came to this form. That the latter form is now used in the sense of a warning sound, and especially in the sense of a sound of trumpet or drum to announce the coming of a military body or the escort of importance affords a good example of the manner in which synonyms are established in the language. A quotation or two may help to fix the word in mind:

> Our stern alarums changed to merry meetings—"Richard III," *i*, 1.

> And when she speaks, is it not an alarum to love?— "Othello," *ii*, 3.

> The dread alarum should make the earth quake to its centre.— Hawthorne, "Old Manse."

*Kerns and gallowglasses, ii*, 13. It may be enough to give simply the fact that the first of these uncouth words means light-armed and the second heavy-armed Irish troops. If the teacher likes, however, he may add a brief mention of the passage from Barnabie Riche:

> The *Galloglas* succeedeth the Horseman, and hee is commonly armed with a skull,[10] a shirt of maile, and a *Galloglas* axe; his service in the field is neither good against horsemen, nor able to endure an encounter of pikes, yet the Irish do make great account of them. The *Kerne* of Ireland are next in request, the

______________

10  A metal covering for the head: a helmet.

very drosse and scum of the countrey, a generation of villaines not worthy to live: these be they that live by robbing and spoiling the poor countreyman, that maketh him many times to buy bread to give unto them, though he want for himself and his poore children. These are they that are ready to run out with every rebell, and these are the very hags of hell, fit for nothing but for the gallows.—*New Irish Prognostication.*

*Thane*, ii, 45. This word may be made interesting by its close connection with the Anglo-Saxon. *Thegan* was originally a servant, then technically the king's servant, and so an Anglo-Saxon nobleman and one of the king's more immediate warriors.

*Bellona*, ii, 54. The mythological allusion is of course easy to handle.

*Composition*, ii, 59. This I would include in the list chiefly to emphasize how often a little common sense will solve what at first sight seems a difficulty of language. "Craves composition" is so easily connected with "composing difficulties" or any similar phrase that an intelligent pupil can see the point if he is only alive to the force of language.

*Aroint*, iii, 6. It will interest most scholars to learn that this word—except for modern imitations—is found only in Shakespeare, and in him but twice, both times in the phrase "Aroint thee, witch" (the second instance, "Lear," iii, 4). They will be at least amused by the possibility of its being derived from a dialect word given in the Cheshire proverb quoted by an old author named Ray in 1693, and probably in use in the time of Shakespeare: "Rynt you, witch,' quoth Bessie Locket to her mother;" and in the speculation whether the dramatist himself made the word. The curious derivation of the term from rauntree or rantry, the old form of rowan, or mountain-ash, is sure to appeal to children who have seen the rowan ripening its red berries. The mountain-ash, or the "quicken," as it is called in

Ireland, is one of the most famous trees in Irish tradition, and is sacred to the "Gentle People," the fairies. It was of old regarded as a sure defence against witches, and the theory of some scholars is that the original form of the exclamation given by Shakespeare was "I've a rauntree, witch," "I've a rowan-tree, witch." All that it is necessary for the reader to know is that the word is evidently a warning to the witch to depart; but there can be no objection to introducing into this preliminary study of the vocabulary matter which is likely to arrest attention and to fix meanings in the mind.

*Rump-fed ronyon, iii*, 6. It is hardly worth while to do more with this than to have it understood that "ronyon" is a term of contempt, meaning scabby or something of the sort, and that "rump-fed," while it may refer to the fact that kidneys, rumps, and scraps were perquisites of the cook or given to beggars, probably indicates nothing more than a plump, over-fed woman.

*Pent-house lid, iii*, 20. A pent-house is from the dictionary found to be a sloping roof projecting from a wall over a door or window; and from this to the comparison with the eyebrow is an easy step. That the simile was common in the sixteenth century may be shown by numerous quotations, as, for instance, the passage in Thomas Decker's "Gull's Horne-book," 1609:

> The two eyes are the glasse windows, at which light disperses itself into every roome, having goodlie pent-houses of hair to overshadow them.

In the second chapter of "Ivanhoe":

> Had there not lurked under the pent-house of his eye that sly epicurean twinkle.

And so on down to our own time, when Tennyson, in "Merlin and Vivian," writes:

He dragged his eyebrow bushes down, and made

A snowy pent-house for his hollow eyes.

*Insane root, iii,* 84. In Plutarch's "Lives," which in the famous translation of North was familiar to Shakespeare and from which he took material for his plays, we are told that the soldiers of Anthony in the Parthian war were forced by lack of provisions to "taste of roots that were never eaten before; among which was one that killed them, and made them out of their wits." Any intelligent student would be likely to understand the force of this phrase from the context, but it is well to speak of it beforehand to avoid distraction of the attention in reading.

*Coign, vi,* 7. "Jutty," from our common use of the verb "to jut," carries its own meaning, and the use of the word "coign" in this passage is given in the "Century Dictionary."

*Sewer, vii, stage-directions.* The derivation and the meaning are also given in the "Century Dictionary," with illustrative quotations.

So far for single words which would be likely to bother the ordinary student in reading. The list might be extended by individual teachers to fit individual cases, and such words included as choppy, *iii,* 44; blasted, *iii,* 77; procreant, *vi,* 8; harbinger, *iv,* 45; flourish, *iv, end*; martlet, *vi,* 4; God 'ield, *vi,* 13; trammel up, *vii,* 3; limbec, *vii,* 67. It is well, however, not to make the list longer than is absolute necessary; and as the vocabulary of the whole play is to be taken up, it is better to trust to the general intelligence of the class as far as possible.

II

These doubtful or obsolete words having been mastered by the class, and the lines in which they occur used as illustrations of their use, the next matter is to take up obscure passages. These may be blind from unusual use of familiar words or from some other cause.

Where the difficulty is a matter of diction it is hardly worth while to make further division into groups, and in the first act the following passages may be given to the students to study out for themselves if possible, or to have explained by the teacher if necessary:

Say to the king *the knowledge of the broil*

As thou did leave it.—*ii*, 6.


For brave Macbeth—well he deserves that name—

*Disdaining fortune*, with his brandished steel

Which smoked with *bloody execution*,

Like *valour's minion* carved out his passage

Till he faced the slave;

Which ne'er shook hands, nor bid farewell to him,

Till he *unseam'd him from the nave to chaps*,

And fix'd his head upon our battlements.—*ii*, 16-23.


Except they meant to bathe in reeking wounds,

Or *memorize another Golgotha*,

I cannot tell.—*ii*, 39-41.


Till that *Bellona's bridegroom, lapp'd in proof,*

*Confronted him with self-comparisons,*

*Point against point rebellious*, arm 'gainst arm,

Curbing his lavish spirit.—*ii*, 54-57.


He shall live a man *forbid.*—*iii*, 21.


The weird sisters, hand in hand,

*Posters* of the sea and land.—*iii*, 32, 33.

Art not without ambition, but without
*The illness should attend it.*—*v*, 20-21.

All that impedes thee from the *golden round*
That fate and *metaphysical aid* doth seem
To have thee crowned withal.—*v*, 30-31.

To *beguile* the time
Look like the time.—*vi*, 63.

—Those honors deep and broad wherewith
Your majesty loads our house: for those of old
And the late dignities heap'd up to them
We rest your *hermits*.—*vi*, 16-20.

This Duncan
Hath borne his *faculties* so meek.—*vii*, 16-17.

What cannot you and I perform upon
The unguarded Duncan? what not put upon
His *spongy* officers, who shall bear the guilt
Of our great *quell*.—*vii*, 69-72.

This list again may be made longer or shorter, with the same proviso as before, that it be not unnecessarily distended. Phrases like "craves composition" and "insane root," which I have put into the first section, may be grouped here if it seems better. I have not felt it needful to indicate the way in which the meaning of these obscure passages is to be brought out, for the method would be essentially the same as that taken to interest the class in the vocabulary of detached words.

**III**

Passages possibly obscure from the thought may for the most part be left for the later study of the play in detail. A few of them it is well to take up for the simple purpose of training the student in poetic language, and some need to be understood for the sake of the first general effect. In the first act of "Macbeth" the passages which it is actually necessary to examine are few, but the list may be made long or short at the pleasure of the teacher. The following may serve as examples:

> The merciless Macdonwald—
>
> Worthy to be a rebel, for to that
>
> The multiplying villainies of nature
>
> Do swarm upon him.—*ii*, 9-12.

> As whence the sun 'gins his reflection
>
> Shipwrecking storms and direful thunders break,
>
> So from that spring whence comfort seem'd to come
>
> Discomfort swells.—*ii*, 25-28.

> But thither in a sieve I'll sail,
>
> And like a rat without a tail,
>
> I'll do, I'll do and I'll do.—*iii*, 8-10.

This passage is a good example of what may be passed over in the first reading, yet which if understood adds greatly to the force of the effect. If the scholar knows that according to the old superstition a witch could take the form of an animal but could be identified by the fact that the tail was wanting, the idea of the hag's flying through the air on the wind to the tempest-tossed vessel bound for Aleppo, and on it taking the form of a tailless rat to gnaw, and gnaw, and gnaw till the ship springs a leak, is sure to appeal to the youthful imagination.

My thought, whose murder yet is but fantastical,

Shakes so my single state of man that function

Is smothered in surmise, and nothing is

But what is not.—*iii*, 139-142.

This is one of those passages which is sure to puzzle the ordinary school-boy, although a little help will enable him to understand it, and to see how natural under the circumstances is the state of mind which it paints. The murder is as yet only imagined (fantastical), and yet the thought of it so shakes Macbeth's individual (single) consciousness (state of man) that the ordinary functions of the mind are lost in confused surmises of what may come as the consequences of the deed; until to his excited fancy nothing seems real (is) but what the dreadful surmise paints, although that does not yet exist.

Your servants ever

Have theirs, themselves, and what is theirs, in compt

To make their audit to your highness' pleasure,

Still to return your own.—*vi*, 25-28.

His two chamberlains

Will I with wine and wassail so convince,

That memory, the warder of the brain,

Shall be a fume, and the receipt of reason

A limbec only.—*vii*, 63-67.

The whole of Macbeth's soliloquy at the beginning of scene *vii* is a case in point. It may be taken up here, but to my thinking is better treated after the class is familiar with the circumstances under which it is spoken.

## IV

The taking up of especially striking passages beforehand may be omitted altogether, although what I consider the possible advantages I have already indicated.[11] Perhaps the better plan is to do this after the first reading of the play, and before the second reading prepares the way for detailed study. The sort of passage I have in mind is indicated by the following examples:

If you can look into the seeds of time,

And say which grain will grow and which will not.—*iii*, 58-59.

The attention of the pupils may be called to the especial force and fitness of the image. The impossibility of telling from the appearance of a seed whether it will grow or what will spring from it makes very striking this comparison of events to them, so unable are we to say which of these "seeds of time" will produce important results and which will show no more growth than a seed unsprouting.

*Dun.* This castle hath a pleasant seat; the air

Nimbly and sweetly recommends itself

Unto our gentle senses.

*Ban.* This guest of summer,

The temple-haunting martlet, does approve

By his loved mansionry that the heaven's breath

Smells wooingly here.—*vi*, 1-7.

This is not only charming as poetry, but it is excellent as a help to train the class to appreciative reading by attention to significant details. "Nimbly,"—with a light, quick motion,—the air "recommends itself,"—comes upon us in a way which makes us appreciate its goodness,—unto our "gentle,"—delicate, capable of

---

11  Page 80.

perceiving subtle qualities,—senses. In the reply of Banquo the use of "guest," one favored and invited, of "temple-haunting," conveying the idea of one frequenting places consecrated and revered, of "loved mansionry," dwellings which the eye loves to recognize, all help to strengthen the impression, and to give the feeling to the mind which we might have from watching the flight of the slim, glossy swallows flitting about their nests.

It is not necessary to multiply examples, since each teacher will have his personal preferences for striking passages; and since many will probably prefer to leave this whole matter to be taken up in the reading.

V

The first reading of a play, whether it come before or after the mastering of the vocabulary, should be unbroken except by the pauses necessary between consecutive recitations, and must above everything be clear and intelligible. In all but the most exceptional circumstances it should be done by the teacher, the class following the text in books of their own. No teacher who cannot read well has any business to attempt to teach literature at all, for reading aloud is the most effective of all means to be used in the study. This does not mean that the reading should be over-dramatic, and still less that it should be what is popularly known as "elocutionary;" but it does mean that it shall be agreeable, intelligent, and sympathetic. The teacher must both understand and feel the work, and must be trained to convey both comprehension and emotion through the voice. The pupils will from a first reading get chiefly the plot, but they may also be unconsciously prepared for the more important knowledge of character which is naturally the next step in the process of studying the drama.

As preparation for the first reading of "Macbeth" little is needed in the way of general explanation. The discussion of the supernatural element, of the responsibility of the characters, and of the central thought of the play, may safely be left for later study. Young people will respond to the direct story, and it is not unwise to let the plot produce its full effect as simple narrative. It is well to state beforehand how it comes that the kingship does not necessarily go by immediate descent, and so to make it evident how Macbeth secured the throne; it may be well also to comment briefly on the state of society in which crime was more possible than now; but beyond this the play may be left to tell its own tale.

In this first reading the teacher will do well to indicate such points of stage-setting as are not evident, and such stage "business" as is necessary to the understanding of the scene. It is as well, however, not to give too much stress to this. To follow the play of emotions is with children instinctive, and this they will do without dwelling on the details of the scene too closely in a material sense. At least a very little aid will be sufficient at this stage. In a subsequent reading these matters may be more fully brought out, although I am convinced that even then it is easy to overdo the insisting upon aids to visualization.

What may be done and should not be omitted is the interspersion in passing of comments so brief that they do not interrupt, yet which throw light upon meanings which might otherwise be likely to pass unnoticed. Nothing should be touched upon in this way which is so complicated as to require more than a word or two to make it plain. What I mean is illustrated by these examples:

> I come Graymalkin.
>
> Paddock calls.—*i*, 9, 10.

The voice in reading conveys the idea that the witches speak to familiar spirits in the air, but it is well to state that fact explicitly.

> What, can the devil speak true?—*iii*, 107.

Banquo thinks instantly of the word of the witches,

Glamis, and thane of Cawdor, etc.—*iii*, 111-119.

In these lines and in 126-147, it is of so much importance that the distinction between the asides and the direct speech be appreciated that it may be well to call attention to the changes.

Cousins, a word, I pray you.—*iii*, 126.

Banquo draws the others aside, probably to tell them of the prediction by the witches of the news they have brought, and this gives Macbeth a moment by himself to think of the strangeness of it.

Think upon what hath chanced.—*iii*, 153.

This is said, of course, to Banquo.

We will establish our estate upon

Our eldest son, Malcolm.—*iv*, 37.

Here the conditions of succession already spoken of may be alluded to, and the fact noted that if Macbeth had entertained any hopes of succeeding Duncan legitimately, these were now dispelled.

And when goes hence?—*v*, 60.

The sinister suggestion of this may well be emphasized by calling attention to it.

By your leave, hostess.—*vi*, 31.

With these words Duncan, who has taken the hand of Lady Macbeth, turns to lead her in.

## VI

Once the play has been read as a whole the way has been prepared for more careful attention to details. For each recitation the parts should be assigned beforehand for oral reading, three or four pupils being assigned to each part so that in a long scene opportunity is given for bringing a number of the students to their feet.[12] It is well to prepare for this second reading by selecting the central motive of the play, and having the class discuss it. In the case of "Macbeth" it is easy to select ambition as the main thread. In some plays a single passion or emotion is not so easily detached, but it is generally needful to remember that if children are to be impressed and are to see things clearly, they must be dealt with simply; so that even at the expense of slighting for the time being some of the strands it is well to keep to the principle of naming one and holding to it with straightforwardness until the work is tolerably familiar.

The children should be made to say—not to write, for contagion of ideas is of the greatest importance here—what they understand by ambition, how far they have noticed it in others, and perhaps how far felt it themselves. A wise teacher should have little difficulty in making such a talk personal enough to enforce the idea without letting it become too intimate. It can be brought out that the test of ambition is the extent of the sacrifices one is willing to make to gratify it. The ambition already spoken of to excel in class, to be at the head of the school baseball nine or football team, to be popular with friends, and so on for the common ambitions of life may seem trifling, but it belongs to the language of the child's life. Here and there the teacher finds pupils who might seize the conception of ambition without starting so near the rudiments, but most need it; I am unable to see how any can be hurt by it. It is much more difficult to get a conception vividly into the minds of twenty pupils together than it is to impress the same thing upon a hundred separately, and I should never feel that I could afford to neglect the humblest means which might be serviceable. The talk, moreover, does not stop here. It is to be led on to what the boys and girls would wish to be in the world; and from this to historic instances of what men have done to gratify their ambitions. The assassination of the late King of Servia is still so recent as to seem much more real than murders farther back in history, and it lends itself

---

12  Personally I would never have a pupil recite except on his feet

well to the effort to make vital the tragedy that is being studied. I am not for an instant urging that literature shall be treated in too realistic a manner, as I hope to show before I conclude; but I do not feel that there is any fear of making it too real to the boys and girls with whom one must deal to-day in our schools.

It is perhaps well, too, that some comment should be made at this stage on the supernatural element. A class is likely to have had geometry by the time it has come to the study of Shakespeare, and most children can with very little difficulty be made to understand that in "Macbeth" and "The Ancient Mariner" the existence of the supernatural is the hypothesis upon which the work proceeds. When this is understood it is not amiss to develop the idea that Shakespeare perhaps introduced the witches as a way of showing how evil thoughts and desires spring up in the heart. The class will easily see that the ideas of ambition, of the possibility of gaining the crown, which little by little grew in the heart of Macbeth can be better shown to an audience by putting the words into the mouths of the witches than by means of soliloquies. This giving of reasons why the dramatist does one thing or another should not be pressed too far and should be touched upon with caution. It is often better to let a detail go unremarked than to run the risk of confusing the mind of the pupil. The witches, however, are almost sure to be remarked upon, and they must be considered frankly.

In this second reading such obscure passages as have been glided over before are to be taken into consideration. If the pupils have, as they should have, texts unencumbered with notes, they may be given a scene or two at a time, and told to use their wits in elucidating the difficulties. Often they show surprising intelligence in this line, and the bestowal of praise where it is deserved is one of the most effective as well as one of the pleasantest parts of the whole process. What they cannot elucidate alone, they may be if possible helped to work out in class, or, if this fails, may be told outright. If they have tried to arrive at the true meaning, they are in a condition when an explanation will have its best and fullest effect.

Passages in the first act of "Macbeth" which I have thus far passed over deliberately, to the end that the pupil be not bothered over too many difficulties at once, are such as these:

Fair is foul, and foul is fair,—*i*, 11.

Where the Norweyan banners flout the sky
And fan our people cold.—*ii*, 49, 50.

Nor would we deign him burial of his men
Till he disbursed, at Saint Colme's inch.—*ii*, 59, 60.

Ten thousand dollars.—*ii*, 62.

If, as is likely to be the case, the greater part or all of the class have passed the word "dollars" without notice, that fact serves to illustrate the need of care in reading. That they should pass it, moreover, illustrates also how the anachronism might pass unnoticed in Shakespeare's time, when historical accuracy was the last thing about which a playwright bothered his head. The teacher may well here refer back to the idea of considering literature as the algebra of the emotions, and remind the class that as the poet was not endeavoring to write history or to tell what happened in a concrete instance, but only to represent the abstract principle of such a situation as that in which Macbeth and his wife were involved, a departure from historical accuracy is of no importance so long as it does not disturb the effect on the mind of the audience or reader.

No more that thane of Cawdor shall receive
Our bosom interest.—*ii*, 63, 64.

I'll give thee a wind.—*iii*, 11.

The supposed power of the witches to control the winds and the superstitions of the sailors about buying favorable weather from them may be taken up in the first reading; but it seems better to leave it for the time when the effect of the play as a whole has been secured, and the interruption will be less objectionable.

His wonders and his praises do contend

Which should be thine or his: silenced with that.—*iii*, 63.

That, trusted home.—*iii*, 120.

Poor and single business.—*vi*, 16.

Like the poor cat i' the adage.—*vii*, 45.

It is not necessary to continue this list. Its length is decided by the one fixed principle to which is no exception: it is too long the moment the teacher fails to hold the interest of the class in the work which is being done. No amount of information acquired or skill in passing examinations can compensate for the harm done by associating the plays of Shakespeare in the minds of the student with the idea of dulness or boredom.

Textual explanation, however, is of small importance as compared to an intelligent grasp of the office and effect of each incident and each scene in the development of the story and of the characters of the actors in the tragedy. At the end of each scene, or for that matter at any point which seems well to the instructor, the students should in this second reading be called upon to comment orally on what has been done in the play and what has been shown. I have much more faith in the genuineness of what a boy says on his feet in the class room than in what he may write at home. A teacher with the gentlest hint may at once stop humbug and conventionality when it is spoken, but when stock phrases, conventional opinions, views imperfectly remembered or consciously borrowed from somebody's notes have been neatly copied out in a theme, no amount of red ink corrects the evil that has been done. The important thing is to get an appreciation, no matter how limited or imperfect it may be, which is yet genuine and intelligent.

With the matter of disputed readings, I may say in parenthesis, the teacher in the secondary school has no more to do than to answer doubts which may arise in the minds of the pupils. Personally I should offer to the consideration of the class the conjectural reading of the line

Vaulting ambition, which o'erleaps itself.—*vii*, 27.

Vaulting ambition, which o'erleaps its selle (saddle);

because it seems to me so plausible and because it is likely to commend itself. For the most part, however, I should let sleeping dogs lie, and if nobody noticed the possible confusion of the text, I would not risk confusion of mind by calling attention to it.

The personal opinions of the class upon the actions and the acts of the characters are not difficult to get at in this way, and often will be the more fully shaped and more clearly thought out if the pupil is constrained to defend an unpopular view. I am not introducing anything new, for this sort of discussion is carried on by every intelligent teacher; it is mentioned here only for the sake of completeness in the process of treating a play in the class-room.

## VII

It may seem superfluous to some teachers to end the study as it began, by a complete, uninterrupted reading of the whole. It is possible that sometimes it would weary a class already weary of going over the same ground; but if so the class has been on the wrong tack throughout. I make the suggestion, however, in confidence that the effect will be good, and that the students will enjoy this review. Whether the reading is done by teacher or pupils depends somewhat upon circumstances; but it should certainly be by the pupils if possible.

# VIII

I have carefully and intentionally omitted all mention of the study of the sources of the plot, the probable date of the play, and things of that sort which interest thorough Shakespearean scholars, and which are the chosen subjects of pedantic formalists. Metrical effects and subtilties are beyond any pupils I have ever encountered in secondary schools. I do not believe that students in the secondary schools should be troubled with any study of this sort. The teacher should of course be prepared briefly to answer any questions of this nature which are put, and to show the pupils where in books of reference information may be found. The great principle is, however, to include in the study nothing which does not enhance the impression of the play as a work of imaginative literature, and to omit everything which can possibly be spared without endangering this general effect.

The danger of overshadowing literary study with irrelevant information is great and constant. The amount of special knowledge which a child must acquire to appreciate a play of Shakespeare's is unhappily large in any case; and the constant aim of the teacher should be to reduce this to a minimum. It is far better that a pupil go through the work with imaginative delight and fail to get the exact meaning of half the obscure passages than that he be bored and wearied by an exact explanation of all of them at the expense of the inspiration of the work as a whole. My painful doubts of the wisdom of our present scheme of insisting upon the study of literature in the common schools arises largely from the unhappy necessity of having so much explained and the too common lack of courage to do a sufficient amount of judicious ignoring of difficulties.

# IX

I cannot shirk entirely, as I should be glad to do, the question of written work on the play we have been considering.[13] It is a

---

13  See chapter xi.

thousand pities that children must be required to write anything about "Macbeth" when they have read it; but it is evident that under existing conditions they will be required to produce something on paper. In regard to this I must repeat that they should never be asked to write as exercises in composition. Everything that a child writes is, in one sense, a rhetorical exercise, but the teacher should impress it upon the class that here the chief aim is to get an expression of the child's thought. The more completely the children can be made to feel that this is not a "composition," but a statement of impressions, of personal tastes, and of opinions, the better.

What subjects are suited for written work is a matter which must be decided by each teacher according to the dispositions, the knowledge, the aptitude shown by the scholars in a particular class. It will inevitably be influenced largely by examination-papers; and in the face of the lists of subjects provided by these it is idle to offer any particular suggestions. In general the test of a subject, so far as real benefit is concerned, is whether it is one upon which the student may fairly be expected to be able to feel and to reason in terms of his own experience. A subject is suited to his needs so long, and so long only, as he is able to consider it as a matter which might concern him personally. He may think crudely and he must of course think inadequately; but he should at least think sincerely and without regard to what somebody else has thought before him. He should be original in the sense that he is putting down his own impressions, is writing thoughts which have not been gathered from books, but have been come at by considering the play in the light of whatever knowledge he personally has of life and human nature.

Much may depend, it is worth remarking, upon the way a subject for theme-work is given out. Phrases count greatly in all human affairs, but especially in the development of children. Adults are supposed to understand words so readily as to be free from the danger of receiving wrong impressions from phraseology which is unfamiliar;

but whether this be true or not, certain it is that the young are often bewildered by words and queerly affected by turns of language. The same theme-subject may be hopelessly incomprehensible or at least unhappily remote when stated in one way, while in another wording it is entirely possible. The first essential is to make clear beyond all possibility of doubt what is required, and this is to be accomplished only by using language which the student understands. The teacher must here as in all instruction keep constantly in mind that language that is clear and familiar to him may be nothing less than cryptic to the class. I remember a lad in a country school who was hopelessly bewildered when confronted with the subject given out by his teacher: "What Character in this Book Appeals to You Most, and on what Grounds?" yet who wrote easily enough a very respectable theme when I said: "She only wants you to pick out the person in the book you like best, and tell why you like him." "Oh, is that all?" he said at first incredulously. "But that isn't saying anything about grounds." The incident, absurd as it is, is really typical.

I have usually found that the word "compare" will reduce most students to mere memories, as they strive almost mechanically to reproduce things set down in the notes of text-books. Nothing is more common than subjects like "Compare the Characters of Macbeth and Lady Macbeth," "Compare 'L'Allegro' and 'Il Penseroso,'" and so on. The result is generally a statement of the criticisms of the characters or works mentioned, a statement which is a poor rehash of notes, but has of real comparison no trace. The comparison calls for analytical powers far beyond anything pupils are likely to have developed; and when a boy asked me not so very long ago what a teacher expected of him when he had been required to compare Sir Roger de Coverley and Will Honeycomb I was forced to reply that I was utterly unable even to conjecture. I regard the frequent appearance of theme-subjects of this sort in the secondary schools with mingled envy and wonder: envy for the teachers who apparently possess the power to elicit satisfactory work on these lines, and wonder that the power to do this work seems so completely to disappear when the pupil leaves the secondary schools.

To comment on the subjects which have actually stood upon entrance examinations in the last half-dozen years would in the first place be invidious, in the second would expose me to an unpleasant danger of seeming to challenge attention to papers for which I have been personally responsible, and in the third place would do no possible good. A teacher with common sense can make the application of the general principles I have stated if he choose; and he will at least minimize the unfortunate necessity of making the written work a preparation for examinations.

**X**

Memorizing is perhaps best done in connection with the last reading of the play, but that is a mere detail. Students should be encouraged to commit to memory the finest passages, and should be given an opportunity of repeating them in the class with as much intelligent effectiveness as possible. They should not, of course, be encouraged or allowed to rant or to "spout" Shakespeare; but the teacher should insist that at least lines be recited so that the meaning is brought out clearly, and he should encourage the speaker to give each passage as if it were being spoken as the expression of a distinct personal thought.

As I said at the beginning of this chapter, I have not endeavored to provide a model, but merely for the sake of suggestiveness to offer an illustration. This is at least one way in which the study of a play may be taken up in the secondary school. Whether it is the best way for a given case is another matter; and I must at the risk of tiresome iteration add that here as everywhere the highest function of the teacher is to discover what is the best possible method not for the world in general, but for the particular class to be dealt with at the moment.

# XIV

# Criticism

What should be used in the way of tests of the knowledge of pupils is a puzzling question for any teacher. Like any other pedagogically natural and necessary inquiry, it can be answered only with a repetition of the caution that no set of hard and fast rules will apply to all schools or to all classes. Students themselves, however, would often be perplexed if they were not given definite tasks to perform, definite questions to answer, definite facts to memorize. In acquiring the vocabulary needed for the reading of a play both teacher and pupil feel with satisfaction that legitimate because tangible work is being done; and for either it is hard to appreciate the fact that the essential thing in the study of literature is too intangible to be tested or measured by specific standards. In what I have called the inspirational treatment of literature both are likely to feel as if a vacation is being taken from real work, since the impression is general that the only method of keeping within the limits of useful educational progress is dependent upon the accomplishing of concrete tasks.

The need of fitting students for examinations is generally allowed in practice to answer the question what shall be done. I have already said that I have personally little faith in the ultimate value of much of the drill thus imposed, and it is hardly to be supposed that any intelligent teacher could be satisfied to let matters rest here. Certainly a pupil who graduates from the high school should have some power of criticising intelligently any book which comes into his hands, and of forming estimates of diction, general form, and to a less extent even of style. His criticism is necessarily incomplete; but it should be genuine and sound as far as it goes. Such a result is not dependent upon the power of passing examinations, but is chiefly secured by precisely that training in appreciation which is least formal and may easily appear farthest from practice in criticism.

Some actual and definite criticism, however, is legitimately a part of the school-work; and concerning this certain things present themselves to my mind as obvious. In the first place criticism is of no value, but rather is harmful, if it fails to be genuine. From this follows the deduction that no criticism can profitably be required until the child is old enough to form an opinion, and that at no stage should comments be asked which are beyond the child's intellectual development. In the early stages criticism is necessarily genuine in proportion as it is personal; and it must have become entirely easy and natural before it can safely be made at all theoretic.

In the early stages of the use of literature in education, as has been said already, the aim is to help the child to enjoy, and to understand so that enjoyment may be inevitable. This should normally be done in the home, but since in a large number of cases in the common schools the effects of home training in literature are so lamentably wanting, the teacher must in most cases undertake to begin at the very beginning. So far as criticism goes, the early stages are of course merely the rudimentary likings or dislikings, and the encouragement of expression of such tastes. Following this comes naturally the putting into word of reasons for preferences. This must be done with simplicity, in the homeliest and most unconventional manner, and above all with no hint to the child that he is doing anything so large as to "criticise." It is precisely at this stage that children are most in danger of contracting the habit of repeating parrot-like the opinions of their elders. All of us have to begin life by receiving the views of adults, and we are all—except in the rare instances of extraordinary geniuses, who need not be much considered here—eager to conceal lack of knowledge by glib repetitions of the ideas of others. To force young pupils to give opinions when they have none of their own to give is to repeat the mistake which Wordsworth notes in his "Lesson for Fathers." The child in the poem unthinkingly declared that he preferred his new home to the old. His father insists upon a reason, and the poor little fellow, having none, is forced into the lie:

"At Kilve there is no weathercock,

And that's the reason why."

In the lower grades the thing which may well and wisely be done is to accustom the children to literature and to literary language. If pupils come to the upper grades and show that this has not been done, the teacher still has it to do, just as he must teach them the alphabet or the multiplication-table if they arrive without the knowledge of these essentials to advanced work. This is the only safe foundation upon which work may rest, and although to acquire it consumes the time which should be put on more elaborate study, that study cannot be soundly done until the rudimentary preparation is well mastered. Criticism must be postponed until the pupil is prepared for it.

Criticism, whenever it come, must begin simply, and it must be connected with the actual life and experience of the child. We are constantly endangering success in teaching by being unwilling to stop at the limits of the possible. Boys and girls will be frank about what they read if they are once really convinced that frankness is what is expected and desired. They are constantly, if not always consciously, on the watch for what the teacher wishes them to say. Whatever encourages them to think for themselves and to state that thought unaffectedly and freely is what is educationally valuable, and this only.

Opinions concerning characters in tales perhaps do as well as anything for the beginning of criticism in classes. A teacher may say to a pupil: "Suppose you had known Silas Marner, what would you have thought of him?" The child is easily led to perceive the difference between seeing or knowing such a man in real life, with its limited chances of any knowledge of character, of the past history of the weaver, of his secret thoughts, or of his feelings, and knowing him from the book which gives all these details so fully. The question then becomes: "Suppose you had in some way found out about him all that the novel tells, what would you have felt?" The teacher will easily detect and should with the gentlest firmness and the firmest gentleness suppress any conventional answers. The young girl who with glib conventionality declares that Silas was a noble character whom she pities because of the way in which he was misunderstood may be questioned whether if she had lived in Raveloe she would have seen more than the homely, unsocial stranger, and whether, even had she known all that was concealed under his homely life, she could have held out against his general unpopularity. She is forced to think when she is asked whether among those who live around her may not be men and women whose lives are as pathetic and as misjudged as was that of the weaver. Children have ideas about the personages in the stories they hear or read, and it is only necessary to encourage, in each pupil according to his temperament, first the formulating of these clearly and then the frank stating of them.

In all this sort of criticism one thing which should be sedulously avoided is any appearance of drawing a moral. Deliberately to draw a moral is almost inevitably to defeat any lesson which the tale might enforce if it is left to make its own effect. The point to be aimed at here is not to turn the story into a sermon, but to make it as close to the individual life of the child as is possible. The difference is in essence that between being told a thing and experiencing it. Once this relation is established, the child feels an emotional share in the matter such as can be created by no amount of sermonizing. It may be doubted if any genuine child ever drew a moral spontaneously, and in all this work spontaneity is the beginning of wisdom.

After the pupil has come to have some notion, more or less clear according to his own mental development, of what the personages in a story or a play are like, he easily goes on to determine the relation of one event to another, the interrelation between the separate parts of the work. He should be able to tell in a general way at least what influence one character has upon another, and of the responsibility of each in the events of the narrative.

These opinions should as much as possible be put into speech before being written. The subject should be talked out, however, in a manner so sincere and straightforward as to make conventionality impossible. Students must be held rigorously to honest and simple expression of real beliefs and feelings. In every class, and perhaps especially among girls, are likely to be some who will surely repeat conventional phrases. Children pick up set phrases with surprising ease, and will offer them whenever they have reason to believe such counterfeit will be received instead of real coin. These shams are easily recognized, and they should be mercilessly dealt with, almost anything except sarcasm, that weapon which is forbidden to the teacher, being legitimate against such cant. The student who repeats a set phrase is usually effectually disposed of by a request to explain, to make clear, and to prove; so that the habit of meaningless repetition cannot grow unless the teacher is insensitive to it. The genuine ideas of the pupils may be developed and put into word in the class, and afterwards the writing out will involve getting them into order and logical sequence.

It may be objected that by this process each scholar will borrow ideas from what he hears said in the class. This is in reality no serious drawback to the method. If the individuals are trained to think for themselves, each will judge the views which are presented in class, and will make them his own by shaping and modifying them. In any case the danger of a student's getting too many ideas is not large, and those he gets from his peers, his classmates, are much more likely to appeal to him and to remain in his mind than any which he culls from books.

The notions will sometimes be crude, but they will be so corrected and discussed in recitation that they cannot be essentially false.

Any criticism which is received from pupils, whether spoken or written, must first of all be intelligent. Sound common sense is the only safe basis for any comment, and the higher the grade of a work of literature imaginatively the more easy is it to treat it in a common-sense spirit. Pupils should be made to feel not only that they have a right to any opinion of their own on what they read, but that they are expected to have one; and that this opinion may be of any nature whatever, so long as they can justify it by sound reasons. Still farther than this, they should be allowed freely to cherish tastes for which they cannot give formal justification—provided they can show a reasonable appreciation of the real qualities of the work they like or dislike. In the higher regions of imaginative work the power of analysis of the most able critic may fail; and it is manifestly idle to expect from school-children exhaustive criticism of high things which yet they may feel deeply.

Since it is of so much importance that all comment and criticism shall be sincere, care must be taken to keep work within limits which make sincerity possible. Students must not be required to perform tasks which are in the nature of things impossible. To push beyond dealing with comparatively simple matters in a frank and direct manner, is inevitably to encourage the use of conventional phrases and to replace sincerity with cant.

A nice question connects itself with the determination of how much it is proper and wise to require of children: it is how much farther it is well to call upon them to criticise literature than we should ask them to comment on life. We need to know what we are doing, and though an examination of the character and motives of a criminal in a book is not the same thing as would be this sort of criticism applied to a flesh and blood neighbor, the two processes are the same in essence. The better the teacher succeeds in arousing the imagination of the pupil, moreover, the more closely the two approach. We should be sure that we are doing well in requiring of the young, who would not and should not be encouraged to dwell on actual crime and suffering, that they produce original opinions upon these things as represented in fiction.

It is of course to be allowed that no teaching can make fictions vital and real in exactly the same way as is that which is known actually to have happened. An imaginative child vitalizes the story which touches him, but does not bring it home to himself as he would occurrences within the circle of his own experience. It may be urged that by encouraging him to analyze sin in the comparatively remote world of fancy we give him a chance to perceive its moral hatefulness without that distrust of his fellows which might come if he were forced to learn the lesson from the harsher happenings of life; and that in books the knowledge of character and circumstance is so much fuller than it is likely to be in experience that he is able to see more clearly. The fact remains, however, that we should hardly expect or desire a lucid and reasonable estimate of the late King and Queen of Servia from the school-children who are being made to write laborious reams on the motives and the character of Macbeth and Lady Macbeth; that we should be shocked at finding boys and girls considering in real life occurrences like the seduction of Olivia Primrose, or suspicions like those Gareth entertained of Lynette. We certainly cannot afford to be prurient, or to confine the young to goody-goody books. They may generally be safely trusted, it seems to me, to read any tale or poem of first-class merit, although its subject were as painful as that of "Œdipus." They will receive it as they receive facts of life told by a wholesome-minded person, often with very little real perception of the darkest and most sinister side. It will be as it was with young Copperfield when he read Fielding's masterpiece and took delight in the hero, "a child's Tom Jones, a harmless creature." When it comes to the discussion of motives, of character, of black events in fiction, the case is different. The child is forced to take a new attitude; to accumulate the opinions of his elders, to view life from their more sophisticated point of view; and inevitably to receive a fresh, and not always a desirable insight into evil. I am not inclined to dogmatize on this point, and touch upon it chiefly for the sake of suggesting that teachers may do well to keep it a little in mind. Each case, it seems to me, must be decided upon its own merit, and I at least have no arbitrary rules to lay down. Of one thing, however, I am sure, and that is that whatever is taken up at all should be treated with absolute and fearless frankness.

All criticism of diction, style, or whatever belongs to literary workmanship necessarily comes late. In the secondary schools I believe very little can profitably be done in this line at all. Of this I shall speak later in connection with the study of workmanship, but here I may say that I suppose most teachers to recognize the obvious absurdity of such questions about metres and metrical effects as are given on page 43. That they should be gravely proposed in a book of advice is indication that somebody believes in them; but any class of students with which I have ever had to deal would be reduced to mechanical repetition of cant conventionality by the bare sight of such interrogations.

One thing which is of importance is the need of encouraging pupils to judge of any work as a whole. It is so much easier to deal with details than with a complete work that constantly students leave schools where the training is in many respects excellent, and have gained no ability to go beyond the examination of particulars. The far more important power of estimating a book or a play from its total effect has not been cultivated. No teacher should forget that the ability to deal fairly with a whole is of as much more value than any facility in minute criticism as that whole is greater than any of its parts.

This does not mean that a student can well summarize everything he reads or that he may wisely attempt it. It does imply that at least his attention shall have been directed over and over to the great fact that the study of details is not the study of a masterpiece; that he shall have been required to judge a book or a play, so far as he is able, as a whole work and with reference to its entire effect. In talking with undergraduates even about short works, pieces no longer than a single essay of Steele or a simple lyric, I constantly find that they are apt to have no conception whatever that they could or should do anything but pick out minute details. I ask what it amounts to as a whole, how it justifies itself, or what is its value as a complete poem or essay, and they seem utterly unable to see what I am driving at. The painful attempt to find out what I wish them to say so entirely occupies their minds as to render them incapable of using whatever power of judgment they may possess. Not long ago one boy said to me: "I didn't know it made any difference what the poem was about if you could pick out things in it." "What do you suppose it was written for?" I asked. A look of painful bewilderment came into his face, and he answered that he supposed some folks liked to write that way. I inquired whether he would test a bridge—he was an engineering student—by picking out bits without seeing how the parts held together and how strong it was as a whole, and he returned with puzzled frankness: "But a bridge has a use." "Very good," was what I assured him, "and so does a poem. Can't you appreciate that mankind has not been keeping poems from generation to generation without finding out if they really are useless? Any work of literature that is really good must be of value as a whole, and you have not got hold of it until you are able to see what it is for as a single thing, a complete unit." The fact is so evident that it seems almost absurd to mention it in a book intended for teachers, but scores of boys come yearly from the fitting-schools who prove how often the fact is ignored,—ignored, very likely, because it is taken for granted, but no less ignored with seriously ill effects.

In general, criticism in the secondary schools should have to do only with the good points of work. Unless a pupil himself shows that he perceives shortcomings in what is read, it is on the whole the place of the instructor to keep the attention of the class fixed on merits, while defects are ignored. This is not to be interpreted as meaning that any weakness should ever be allowed to pass for a merit; or as indicating that it is ever wise to shirk a difficulty. Any intelligent pupil, for instance, should see for himself that the metaphors are sadly and inexcusably mixed in the passage:

> Whether 'tis nobler in the mind to suffer
>
> The slings and arrows of outrageous fortune,
>
> Or to take arms against a sea of troubles,
>
> And by opposing end them.

It is necessary to meet this knowledge frankly, and to show him how it is that Shakespeare can be so great in spite of faults like this. It is the inclination of childhood to feel that a man must be perfect to be great, but even at the cost of encountering the difficulty of such a faith the truth must be told. In general, however, it is as well not to go out of the way to enforce the doctrine of human fallibility, and the youthful mind is best nourished by being fed on what is good, rather than by being taught to perceive what is bad.

When a pupil is asked to put into words the reason why a piece is written, he should be required to answer by a complete sentence, a properly phrased assertion. He is not unlikely to begin by giving a single term, an incomplete and tentative phrase, or at best a fragmentary statement. For the sake of the clearness of his own idea and of the habit of accurate thinking, he should be encouraged and expected to make the idea clear and the statement finished. Student-criticism, as I have said perhaps often enough already, cannot in the nature of things be either profound or exhaustive, but it should be intelligent and well defined as far as it goes.

# XV

# Literary Workmanship

The appreciation of literary workmanship dawns very slowly on the child's mind. In the secondary schools not much can be accomplished in the way of making students feel the niceties of literary art; but something should be done to enforce the nature and the worth of technique. Much that touches the undergraduate's feelings he cannot analyze, and should never in any work of the secondary schools be asked to criticise. He should, however, if he is to be systematically trained in the study of masterpieces, have knowledge enough of the qualities which distinguish them from lesser work to perceive on what their claims to superiority are founded. Children so naturally and so generally feel that distinctions which do not appeal to them are arbitrary, and it is of so much importance to guard against any feeling of this sort in the case of literature, that it is worth while to be at some pains to make distinctions perceptible, even if they may not always be made entirely clear.

One of the tests of rank in civilization is appreciation of workmanship. The savage knows nothing of mechanics beyond the power of a lever in prying up a rock, the action of a bowstring, or crude facts of this sort. A machine to him is not only incomprehensible, but supernatural: a locomotive is a fire-devil, and a loom or a printing-press, should he see one, a useful spirit. At the other end of the scale of appreciation of mechanical appliances is the inventor who devises or the trained engineer who understands the most complicated engines of modern ingenuity. Somewhere between stands any one of us,—the ordinary pupil presumably far above the savage, but far below the expert. In the appreciation of the art of the painter, at the bottom of the scale is the bushman who can look at the clever painting of a man and not know what it represents, and at the top the great painters of the world and those who can best enter into the spirit of their productions. In this scale again each of us stands somewhere; the average school-boy is unhappily likely to be so far down as to take delight in the colored illustrations of the Sunday newspapers and to be utterly indifferent to a Titian or a Rembrandt. In comprehension of the value and effect of language, the same principle obtains. The scale extends from the savage tribes with a vocabulary of but a few hundred words for the entire speech of the race and no power of making combinations beyond the simplest, to the cultivated nations with perhaps a couple of hundred thousand words and the art of producing the highest forms of prose and of poetry. The scale is a long one, and its development has taken uncounted ages; but somewhere in the line each individual has his place. The degree of the civilization of a race is unerringly determined by its command of the written word; the mental rank of the individual is no less certainly fixed by his power of using and of comprehending human speech.

This general truth is easily brought home to young people by reminding them how they began their knowledge of language with the acquirement of single words and went on to appreciate how much more may be expressed by word-combinations. After the infantile "give" came in turn "p'ease give" and "please give me a drink." From such stages each of them has gone on learning. They have constantly increased their vocabulary, their knowledge of the value of words, of word-arrangement, and of sentence-construction. Gradually by practical experience they have gained some appreciation of all those points which make up the sum of instruction in classes in composition. They now need to be shown that literary appreciation is the extension of this knowledge along the same lines; that it is the means of advancing toward a higher place in that scale which extends from the ignorant savage to the sages. They may in this way be brought to a conception of literary technique as a matter connected with the process of perception which they have been carrying on from childhood.

How value in all workmanship is to be judged by the effects produced is admirably illustrated by machinery, but it is hardly less evident in the case of language. The simpler forms of sentence come to be used by the child in place of single disconnected words because with sentences he can do more in the way of communicating his ideas and obtaining what he desires. To illustrate more complicated forms of language we have only to remind the child how carefully he orders his speech when he is endeavoring to coax a favor from an unwilling friend or a reluctant parent. The child feels himself clever just in proportion as he is able so to frame his plea that it secures his end. He may be reminded that he selects most carefully the terms which suggest such things and ideas as favor his wish and avoids any that might hint at possible objections. Out of these homely, universal experiences of childhood it is possible to build up in the mind of the pupil a very fair notion of the nature and the use of literary workmanship; a notion, moreover, which is at once sound in principle and entirely adequate as a working basis.

Teaching consists principally in helping pupils to extend ideas which they have received from daily life. In this matter of literary workmanship, for instance, it means showing them that they have, without being especially conscious of the fact, a responsiveness to well-turned forms of speech and to skilful use of words. They may perhaps be made to appreciate this with especial vividness by having their attention called to the pleasure they take in clever or apt sayings from their fellows or from joking speeches. This form of illustration must, it is true, be used with discretion. It is always difficult to lead the mind of a child from the concrete to the general. Not a few children—and children, too, of considerable intelligence—are not unlikely, if jesting remarks are instanced, to conclude that good literary workmanship means something amusing. With due care, however, a class may be led to see how the same quality of apt presentation in word which pleases them in the sayings of schoolmates is what, carried farther, is the foundation of literary technique.

Concrete examples of thoughts so well expressed that they have come to be almost part of common speech are abundant. The crisp, dry phrases of Pope lend themselves admirably as illustration, they are so neat, so compact, and, it may be added, so free from delicate sentiment which might be blurred in the handling.

Order is heaven's first law.

An honest man's the noblest work of God.

The class can supply examples in most cases, and be pleased with itself for being able to do so. The finer instances from greater writers may be led up to, the epigrams of Emerson, the imaginative phrases of Shakespeare; and so on to longer examples, with illustrations from the rolling paragraphs of Macaulay, the panoplied prose of De Quincey, and after that from lyrics and passages in blank verse. Thus much may be done in the way of instruction in technique fairly early in high-school work. With it or after it at a proper interval should follow instruction in regard at least to the mechanical differences between prose and poetry and what they mean. I have mentioned earlier[14] the impression students often bring from the reading of Macaulay's "Milton." The remarks there quoted are selected from answers to a question of an entrance paper in regard to the difference in form and in quality between prose and poetry. Others from the same examination show yet more strikingly the general haziness of conception in the minds of the candidates:

> In prose words are thrown together in a way to make good sense and to form good English. Poetry is the grouping of words into a metric [*sic*] system.

---

14   Page 36.

Poetry is often written in rhyme, while prose is expressed in sentences.

Poetry is the name given to writing that is written in verse form. One does not as a rule get the meaning of things when they are written in verse form.

Prose may be verse when dealt with by such an author as Shakespeare or Milton, but prose usually consists of words arranged in sentences and paragraphs without any special order.

Poetry is used as a pastime, and as such is all right.

Between good blank verse and prose there is not much difference except in the form of wording in which it is put upon the page.

For me, the difference between prose and poetry is this: Prose does not rhyme and poetry does. Under such a definition, all literature not poetry must be prose. Therefore Shakespeare's works are prose.

The illustrations might be much extended, but these will show the confusion which existed in the minds of boys who had been painfully drilled in the college entrance requirements. I have not selected the examples for their absurdity, although in a melancholy way they are droll enough; but I have meant them to illustrate the confusion which existed in the minds of a large number of the candidates at that particular examination of what makes the vital difference between prose and poetry. It is not my contention that teachers in the secondary schools are to go into minute details in regard to poetic form; but I do believe that it is idle to talk about the rank of a writer as a poet or of the beauty of Shakespeare's verse to students who do not know the difference between verse and prose.

I may be allowed to remark in passing that to my mind the influence of the theories of Macaulay's "Milton" alluded to above illustrates the difference in effect of that which appeals to the personal experience and feelings of boys and that which they are forced to receive without such inward interpretation. The boys who were trained in the "Milton" were trained also in Carlyle's "Burns." The Carlyle, with its eloquent appreciation of the office of the poet, the seer to whom has been given "a gift of vision," had apparently left no trace upon their minds. They had, however, been forced, too often unwilling, over numerous pages of what they were assured was poetry of the highest quality, yet which to them was unintelligible and wearisome. When Macaulay declared that poetry was a relic of barbarism they seized upon the theory eagerly because it justified their own feelings, because it coincided with their own impressions; and thenceforth they doubtless held complacently to their faith in the obsolete uselessness of verse, fortified by so high an authority.

In the whole body of papers in the examination from which I have been quoting very few gave the impression that the writer had a clear conception that somehow, even if he could not express it, a vital difference exists between poetry and prose. The greater number of the boys seemed to think that rhyme made the distinction, or that distortion of sentences was the leading characteristic. Not one teacher in a score had succeeded in impressing upon his pupils the fundamental truth that the only excuse poetry can have for existing is that it fulfils an office impossible for prose. Yet nothing which can properly be called the study of poetry can be done until this prime fact is recognized with entire clearness. Beyond the entirely unanalytical enjoyment of verse, the native responsiveness to rhythm, and the uncritical pleasure with which one learns to love literature and to seek it as a means of pleasure, the first, the most primary, the absolutely indispensable fact to be thoroughly impressed on a young student is that poetry uses form as a part, and an essential part, of its language. The boy must be made to understand that just as he tries by his tone, by his manner, by his smile, to produce in his hearers the mood in which he wishes them to receive what he has to say, so the poet by his melody, by the form of his verse, by his ringing rhythms or long, melting cadences, by his rhyme or his pauses, is endeavoring to interpret the ideas he expresses as surely as he is by the statements he makes. The truth which the teacher knows, that not infrequently the metrical effect is really of more value and significance than the ideas stated, is naturally for the most part too deep for the comprehension of pupils at this stage. It would only confuse a class to go so far as this; but if we are to "study" poetry, we must have at least a working definition of what poetry is, and one which shall commend itself to the children with whom we are working.

As a mere suggestion which may be of practical use to some teachers, I would call attention to what may be done by comparing certain pieces of prose with the poems which have grown out of them. I know of nothing better for this use than Tennyson's "Ballad of the Revenge" and the prose version of Sir Walter Raleigh from which it is taken. In many parts the language is almost identical,—but with the differences between robust prose and a stirring lyric. The teacher who can make a class see what the distinction is, what the ballad accomplishes that Raleigh has not attempted, will have made clear by concrete example what poetry does and why it is written. Another example is Byron's "Destruction of Sennacherib" compared with the original version of the incident as given in the Bible.

It may seem to some teachers that I am going rather deep, but to such I should simply propound the question what they understand by the study of poetry. The natural error of the untrained mind is to regard the intellectual content of a poem as its reason for being, and to foster such an error as this is to make forever improbable if not impossible any intelligent or genuine insight into poetry whatever. If we are not to protect children against this mistake, fatal as it is to any perception of the real province and nature of poetic art, what do we expect to accomplish in all the extensive attention which is under the present system devoted to the works of the masters?

That so many boys failed to answer satisfactorily in this matter of distinguishing between prose and poetry is of course not conclusive evidence either of general ignorance or of conscious fault on the part of instructors. Boys often fail in attempts to state distinctions about which they are yet reasonably clear in their minds, and it may well be that many who gave absurd replies would have no difficulty in discriminating between verse and prose,—at least when verse fulfilled the specification of the candidate who wrote:

> A jagged appearance is the main form-characteristic of blank verse. Each sentence is a separate line, and every other sentence is indented about a quarter of an inch.

It would be interesting to present to pupils who have finished the study of the college requirements half a dozen brief selections, some prose and some poetry, but all printed in solid paragraphs. The number of students who could accurately and confidently distinguish in every case would be a not unfair test of the extent to which the distinction is understood.

Teachers probably fail to make this matter clear because they not unnaturally assume that of course any intelligent lad in his teens must know the distinction between prose and poetry. Natural as such an assumption may be, however, it is often—indeed, I am tempted to say generally—wrong. The chief business of the modern teacher is after all the instructing of pupils in things which they would naturally be supposed to know already. It is certainly safer never to assume in any grade that a student knows anything whatever until he has given absolute proof. The weakest points in the education of the modern student are certainly those which are continually taken for granted.

One of the most serious obstacles in the way of bringing young people to understand technical excellence and to appreciate literary value is the difficulty of having school-work done with proper deliberation. It is doubtful if any process in education can profitably be hurried; it is certain that nothing of worth can be done in the study of literature which is not conducted in a leisurely manner. The first care of an instructor in this delicate and difficult branch must be to insure a genial atmosphere: an atmosphere of tranquillity and of serenity. No matter how tall a heap of prescribed books may block the way to the end of the school year, each masterpiece that is dealt with should be treated with deference and an amount of time proportioned not to its number of pages but to the speed with which the class can assimilate its worth and beauty. If worst comes to worst, I would have a teacher say honestly to his pupils: "We have taken up almost all of the term by treating what we have studied as literature instead of huddling through it as a mechanical task. For the sake of examinations we are forced to crowd the other books in. The process is not fair to them or to you; so do not make the mistake of supposing that this is the proper way of treating real books." Children who have been properly trained will understand the situation and will appreciate the justice of the proposition.

In this connection is of interest the remark of an undergraduate who said that he obtained his first impression of style and of the effectiveness of words from translating. "I suppose the truth is," he explained with intelligence, "that in English I never read slowly enough to get anything more than the story or what was said. When I was grubbing things out line by line and word by word I at last got an idea of what my teachers had meant when they talked about the effect of the choice of words." Many of us can look back to the days when we learned grammar from Latin rather than from English, although we had been over much the same thing in our own tongue. In the foreign language we had to go deliberately and we had to apply the principles we learned. Only when the student is treating literature so slowly and thoroughly that these conditions are reproduced does he come to any comprehension of style or indeed of the real value of literature.

Readers of all ages naturally and normally read anything the first time for the intellectual content: for the story, for the information, for that meaning, in short, which is the appeal to the intellectual comprehension. The great majority are entirely satisfied to go no farther. They do not, indeed, perceive the reason for going farther; and they are too often left in ignorance of the fact that they have entirely missed the qualities which entitle what they have read to be considered literature in the higher sense.

In this they are often encouraged, moreover, by the unhappy practice of making paraphrases. The paraphrasing of masterpieces is to me nothing less than a sacrilege. It degrades the work of art in the mind of the child, and contradicts the fundamental principle that poetry exists solely because it expresses what cannot be adequately said in any other way. A paraphrase bears the same relation to a lyric, for instance, that a drop of soapy water does to the iridescent bubble of which it was once the film. The old cry against the selection of passages from Milton for exercises in parsing should be repeated with triple force against the use of literature as material for children to translate from the words of the poet into their own feeble phraseology. The parsing was by far the lesser evil. It is often necessary to have an oral explanation of difficult passages; but this should be always expressly presented as simply a means to help the child to get at the real significance of a lyric, a sort of ladder to climb by. Any paraphrasing and explaining should be carefully held to its place as an inadequate and unfortunate necessity. The class should never be allowed to think that any paraphrase really represents a poet, or that it is to be regarded in any light but that of apologetic tolerance.

In this matter of workmanship, as everywhere else in the process of dealing with literature, much depends upon the character of the class. Much must always be left unaccomplished, and much is always wisely left even unattempted. Often the teacher must go farther in individual cases than would naturally have been the case in a given grade because questions will be asked which lead on. It is often necessary, for instance, to explain that the crowding forward of events made unavoidable by stage conditions is not a violation of truth, but a conforming to the truth of art. A lad will object that things could not move forward so rapidly, and it is then wise to show him that dramatic truth does not include faithfulness to time, but may condense the events of days into an hour so long as it is true to human nature and to the effects those events would have had if occurring at intervals however great. Again children will object in a tale that the incidents are not likely to have happened; and it is then necessary to make clear the distinction between probability and possibility, and how fiction may deal with either. These matters, however, are to be left to the intelligence of the individual instructor. If he cannot manage them wisely without advice, he cannot do it with arbitrary rules.

For a last word on the matter of training students in the appreciation of literary form and workmanship I should offer a warning against attempting too much. Something is certainly unavoidable, but of minutiæ it is well to exercise what Burke calls "a wise and salutary neglect." Literary language must be learned or all intelligent work is utterly impossible; since form is an important element in all artistic language, it is not possible to ignore this. The extent to which work can and should go in the study of form in a given class is one of the matters which the instructor has to decide; and when he has decided it he must resolutely refuse to allow himself to be unhappy because in the great realm of literature are so many noble tracts of which he has not even hinted to his class the existence. If he has done the lesser work well he has at least put his students in a condition to do the greater for themselves; if he had attempted more he might have accomplished nothing.

# XVI

# Literary Biography

How far the biography of authors shall be a part of the school-work is a question which deserves attention. I began these talks by calling attention to the fact that it is so much easier to teach details about the life of a writer than it is to train the youthful mind to a true appreciation of literature itself. Teachers naturally and almost unconsciously fall into the habit of over-emphasizing this division of the history of literature, and questions about the lives of authors are dangerously easy to formulate for recitation or for examination-paper. Nothing, however, should be allowed to obscure the idea that the work and not the worker is the thing with which study should be concerned; and everybody would agree that in theory the limit to biographical inquiry in secondary-school study is the extent to which a knowledge of an author's career or personality aids to the understanding of what he has written.

To say this, however, is much like restating the question. Like a good deal that passes for argument, it only puts the problem in other words; for we are at once confronted with the doubt how far a pupil in the secondary school is likely to be helped by knowing about the facts of a writer's life. At the beginning of the "Spectator" Addison remarks:

> I have observed that a reader seldom peruses a book with pleasure,
> till he knows whether the writer of it be a black or a fair man, of
> a mild or choleric disposition, married or a bachelor, with other

particulars of the like nature, that conduce very much to the right understanding of an author.

I may frankly confess that this is so entirely untrue of myself that I am perhaps not a fair judge for others. Since it is to me a matter almost of indifference who wrote a book, where or when he lived, what he was and what he did, I have not perhaps estimated rightly the effect of biography on children. I am firm in my belief, however, that for making literature more clear, more vivid, more attractive, the effect of a knowledge of the author's life is with children apt to be practically nothing. If they are interested in a book, they may on that account like to know something of the man who wrote it, but I have yet to find a student who really cared for a piece of literature because he had been made to learn facts about the author. That a book was written in a given age will account to him for fashions of thought strange to-day, but he is seldom able to carry such analysis beyond the most general idea.

In regard to helping scholars in the secondary schools to understand a given piece of literature by instructing them about the personality of the writer, I am quite as skeptical. It may be that one lad in a hundred may come to a better appreciation of a book from what he knows of the temperament of the author. It is possible to point this out in occasional striking instances. If a boy read "A Modest Proposal," a teacher naturally calls attention to the character of Swift as having determined the ferocious form which this plea for humanity has taken; in dealing with "The Journal of the Plague Year" it is inevitable that the instructor speak of the journalistic tendency of Defoe, which led him to write on topics which were at the moment before the public. In either case the result is not important in the sense of going much beyond what the student may be made to feel without any mention of the writer or the writer's peculiarities.

It is very easy to delude ourselves into feeling that we are being helpful when in reality we are simply being pedagogic. If our pupils were so far advanced as to be able to perceive the subtle relations between character and literature, between the nature of a writer and the interpretation we are to put upon what he has written, they would in most cases be better fitted to instruct us than to receive any instruction we are able to furnish. It is sometimes well to give pupils things which we are aware they cannot grasp; to show them the existence of lines of thought which they are not yet qualified to carry out. Our aim in this is to broaden their perceptions, and to direct them toward truths which later they may investigate for themselves. In the secondary schools, however, very little of this sort can be profitably done in connection with anything so complex and subtle as the relation of the character of an author to his work. Young people must take literature at its face value, so to say, and in teaching them to do this is more than room for all the energies a teacher in these grades can bring to bear.

The history of literature, its development, its relations to the evolution of human thought, should all be as far as possible familiar to the teacher; and no instructor with knowledge and enthusiasm is likely to ignore any of these in dealing with masterpieces. They must all, however, be brought forward with care, for it is easy to overwhelm the mind of the young, especially in an age like the present when a child goes to school with attention already strained by the imperative and insistent calls of daily life. Students on leaving the high school should be familiar with the place in the centuries of authors they have especially studied, and of the score or so of writers most important in English literature from Chaucer down. With the exact details of biography they need not have been concerned. If they have had curiosity enough to look these up as a matter of individual interest, it is well, although I am not sure that anything is gained by encouraging this research. To know of Shakespeare, of Chaucer, and of Milton, for instance, what may be put into a dozen lines; and of lesser writers to have proportionate information, seems to me ample.

The work and not the worker is of importance; the book and not the author; the poem and not the poet.

Many teachers will not agree with me in giving to the personality and the biographies of writers so small a place. Every man must judge by his own experience, and I can only say that every year I deal with classes in literature I find myself deliberately giving less attention to the history of literature. I have insisted already upon the danger that such study shall take the place of the consideration of literature itself, and I have now attempted to reënforce that thought by stating definitely what it seems to me wise to attempt in the secondary schools. I do not desire to be dogmatic, however, and here as elsewhere the conclusion of the whole matter is that while the question of the wisdom of giving extended instruction in literary history or biography is to be carefully considered, each instructor must frame the answer according to personal experience and the individual needs of any given class.

# XVII

# Voluntary Reading

No teacher who is really concerned with the development of the pupil's mind can afford to ignore outside influences. Indeed, even were a teacher conceivable who, consciously or unconsciously, cared only to drag scholars over the prescribed course, he would yet be forced to take into account the effect of every-day life and circumstance, and under existing conditions every teacher is sure to find that he is to a great extent obliged to do the work of the home in all that relates to the æsthetic training of a large number of children. In teaching literature it is not only wise but it is easy to discover and to a large extent to influence whatever reading pupils do of their own will outside of the required work.

Thoroughly to accomplish all that a teacher desires, or even all that is often expected of him, would be possible only to the gods; and it is evident enough that no instructor can exercise complete parental supervision over all the life of the pupils under him. Certain things in the training of the young are accomplished at home or go forever undone. Perhaps the most serious difficulty in this whole complicated business of education is that the schoolmaster is so largely called upon to undo what is done outside the schoolroom. He may at least be thankful that in the matter of reading he is dealing with something tangible, something in which so many of his flock may with skilful management be influenced.

In a leaflet published under the auspices of the New England Association of Teachers of English, "The Voluntary Reading of High School Scholars," Professor W. C. Bronson, of Brown University, comments on the fact that the mind of the young person is likely to perceive little relation between the literature administered at school and the books voluntarily read outside. He says:

> Many of our high-school youth are leading a double life in things literary: in the class-room Doctor Jekyll studies the lofty idealism of "Comus" or "Paradise Lost;" outside, Mr. Hyde revels in the yellow journalism and the flashy novel; and in many cases Doctor Jekyll does not even realize that he has changed into another and lower being.

The difficulty in making boys and girls realize a connection between school-work and actual life is familiar to every teacher. I am personally convinced that one reason for this—although obviously not the only one—is the modern tendency to diminish the sense of value and necessity by too much yielding to the inclination of the child. Coaxing along the line of the least resistance is sure to produce an effective even if hardly conscious indifference, which is far less healthy than the temper of mind bred by insistence upon progress along the line of duty. Be that as it may, however, the modern scholar generally regards school as one thing and life as practically another. Books read in the class-room, books studied, discussed as a part of formal and required work, are felt to be remote from daily existence and almost as something a bit unreal. They may be even enjoyed, and yet seem to the illogical youthful mind as having a certain adult quality which sets them apart from any vital connection with the life of youth. It is not uncommon, I believe, for a boy to like a book in his private capacity, reading it for simple and unaffected pleasure, and yet to feel it almost a duty to be bored by the same book when it comes up as a part of the work of the school-room.

Very likely a hint of the explanation of the whole matter is to be found in this last fact. In the first place the work of the schoolroom, however gently administered, represents compulsion, and we have trained the rising generation to feel that compulsion is a thing to be abhorred. Perhaps nothing could ever make school-work the same as the life which is voluntary and spontaneous; but modern methods have generally not succeeded in minimizing this difficulty. In the second place, teachers are too often uncareful or unable to soften the differences between reading without responsibility of thoroughness and reading with the consciousness that class-room questionings may lie beyond. Almost any child has the power of treating a book or a poem as a friend when he reads for pleasure and of regarding the same book as an enemy when it becomes a lesson. The thing is normal and not unhealthy; but it is to be reckoned with and counteracted.

Professor Bronson, in his brief discussion of the matter, goes on to remark that where the Jekyll and Hyde attitude of mind exists—which to some degree, I believe, would be in every pupil—

> The first task of the teacher is to make the pupil fully realize it and to urge upon him the necessity of discrimination in his voluntary reading. For this purpose ridicule of trashy books by name and praise of good books, with reasons why they are good, may well fill the part of a recitation period, now and then, even though the routine work suffer a little. For the same purpose, it is very desirable that more of the best modern literature be made a part of the English course, especially in the earlier years, when the pupil's taste is forming, for it is easier to bring such works into close relation with his voluntary reading. The teacher of English may also consider himself recreant if he does not give his class advice about the reading of magazines and instructions how to read the newspapers.

With the spirit of this I agree entirely. The letter does not seem to me entirely satisfactory. I have learned to be a little afraid of ridicule as a means of affecting the minds of the young in any direction. It is the easiest of methods, but no less is it the one which requires the most prudence and delicacy. It is the one which is most surely open to the error of the point of view. If the teacher tries to lessen the inclination of pupils for specific books by ridicule, he can do no good unless he is able to make the class feel that these books are ridiculous not only according to the standards of the teacher but according to the standard of the child. To prove that from the instructor's point of view a book is poor and silly amounts to little if the work really appeals to the young. No more is effected than would be accomplished if the teacher told lusty lads that to him playing ball seemed a foolish form of amusement. They appreciate at once that he is speaking from a point of view which is not theirs and which they have no wish to share. He must be able to make it evident that the book in question, with its attractions, which he must frankly acknowledge, is poor when judged by standards which the pupils feel to be true and which belong to the sphere of boyhood.

I confess with contrition that in my zeal for good literature I have in earlier days spoken contemptuously of popular and trashy books which I had reason to think my boys probably enjoyed and admired. I believe I was wrong. Now I do not hesitate to say what I think about any book when a student asks me, but I make it a rule never in class to attack specific books or authors for anything but viciousness, and that question is hardly likely to arise in the secondary schools. I cannot afford to run the risk of alienating the sympathies of my pupils, and of arousing a feeling that my point of view is so far removed from theirs that they cannot trust my opinions to be sympathetic. The normal attitude of the child toward the adult is likely enough to be that of believing "grown-ups" to be so far from understanding what children really care for as to be entirely untrustworthy in the selection of reading. The child disregards or distrusts the judgments of his elders not on abstract grounds, but merely from an instinctive feeling that adults do not look at things from his point of view. I always fear lest by an unwise condemnation of a book which a lad has enjoyed I may be strengthening this perfectly natural and inevitably stubborn conviction.

The first and most important means of influencing outside reading is by impressing upon the child's mind the idea that he is studying literature chiefly for the sake of reading to himself and for himself. About this should be no doubt or uncertainty. No child should for a moment be allowed to suppose that such dealing with books as is possible in the school-room can be chiefly for its own sake, can be so much an end as a means. To allow him to suppose that the few works he goes over can be held adequately to represent the great literary treasures of the race, or that he can be supposed to do more than to learn how to deal with literature for himself, is at once to make instruction in this branch more an injury than a benefit. It would be no more reasonable than to allow him to think that he learns the multiplication-table for the sake of his school "sums" rather than that he may have an effective tool to help him in the practical affairs of life.

To influence outside work of any sort is difficult, especially in city schools where the pupils are subject to so many distractions. The teacher is generally obliged to make his effort in this direction almost entirely individual, treating no two scholars exactly in the same way, and he is not infrequently obliged to employ a considerable amount of shrewdness in the process. "When I wish to talk to John Smith about his reading," a clever teacher said in my hearing, "I send to him to see me about his spelling, or his handwriting, or anything to give an excuse for a chat. Then I bring in the thing I am aiming at as if by accident." The number of instructors possessed of the adroitness, the time, and the patience for this sort of finesse is probably not large; but much may be done by words dropped apparently by chance, if only the instructor has the matter earnestly at heart.

How far the relation of books in the required reading to books read voluntarily may profitably be insisted upon in class must depend largely upon the particular pupils involved. Every teacher will certainly do well to find out what his students are reading outside, if they are reading anything, and he should then consider what use to make of his knowledge. The very fact that he concerns himself about the matter will call the attention of the class to the fact that a connection exists; and that it is real enough to be worth heeding. Any wise teacher will find an advantage in having indications of the natural tastes and inclinations of those he is trying to train, and to know what the boys and girls really like to read will often correct a tendency to speak of the required readings in a tone that is outside the range of the sympathies of the scholars. If he knows that the girls are fond of weeping over "The Broken Heart of the Barmaid," that the boys revel in "The Bloody Boot-jack," that both find "Mrs. Pigs of the Potato-patch" exquisitely amusing, he sees at once that he must be cautious in dwelling on the pathos of "Evangeline," the romance of "The Flight of a Tartar Tribe," or the humor of Charles Lamb. Children fed on intellectual viands so coarse would find real literature insipid, and must be trained with frank acceptance of that fact.

To say that teachers may also often do something in the way of arousing parents to do their part in guiding the reading of children is to go somewhat outside of my field. The public asks so much of teachers already that any hint of labor in the homes of pupils seems— and in many cases would be—nothing less than the suggestion of an impossibility. If I were to urge the matter, I should do it purely on the ground that teachers may sometimes greatly lessen the difficulty of the task they undertake in the school-room by a little judicious labor in the home. In the public schools to-day many children, perhaps even a majority, come from homes wherein no literary standard is apparent, and where for the most part none exists. They are being given a training which their parents did not have, and they feel themselves better able to direct their elders in things intellectual than their fathers and mothers are to advise them. In these cases, certainly very numerous, the teacher must accept the inevitable, and do what he can by inducing his pupils to talk with him about their outside reading. Where parents are more cultivated, much may often be effected by the simple request or suggestion that the young folk be supervised a little in the choice of books. The teacher must of course use tact in doing anything in this line, especially in those cases where such a request is most needed. Parents who pay least attention to such matters are especially likely to resent interference with their prerogative of neglecting their children, though they may generally be reached by the flattery of a carefully phrased request for coöperation. Few things are more delicate to handle than neglected duties, and the fathers and mothers who shirk all responsibility for the mental training of their offspring must be approached as if they jealously tried to leave nothing in this line for any teacher to do.

The most common fault of young people to-day in connection with reading is the neglect of books altogether or the devouring of fiction of a poor quality. To urge boys and girls to read good books or to admonish them to avoid poor ones is seldom likely to effect much. Such direct and general appeal is sure to seem to them part of the teacher's professional routine work, and not to alter their inclinations or to make any especial difference with their practice. Children are led to care for good reading only by being made acquainted with books that appeal to them; and they are protected against poor or injurious reading only by being given a taste for what is better.

This summing-up of the situation is easily made, but how to make children acquainted in a vital and pleasant fashion with good books and how to cultivate the taste is really the whole problem which we are studying. This is the aim and the substance of all genuine teaching of literature, and everything in these talks is an attempt to help toward an answer. When the problem of voluntary reading has been satisfactorily solved the work of the teacher is practically done, for the pupil is sure to go forward in the right direction whether he is led or not. All that treatment of literature which for convenience

I have called "inspirational" is directly in the line of developing and raising the taste of young readers, and beyond this I do not see that specific rules can be given. Personal influence is after all what tells, and the most that can be done here is to call attention to the fact that in so far as a teacher can influence and direct the voluntary reading of a pupil he has secured a most efficient aid to his school-work in literature.

# XVIII

# In General

Throughout these talks I have tried to deal with the teaching of literature in practical fashion, not letting theory lead me to forget the conditions actually existing. To consider an ideal state of things might be interesting, but it would hardly help the teacher bothered by the difficulties of every-day school-work. I have intended always to keep well within the field of ordinary experience, and to make suggestions applicable to average teaching. How well I have succeeded can be judged better by teachers than by me; but I wish in closing to insist that at least I believe that what I have said is every-day common sense.

I have throughout assumed always that no teacher worthy of the name can be content with merely formal or conventional results, but will be determined that pupils shall be brought to some understanding of what literature really is and of why it is worthy of serious attention—to some appreciation, in a word, of literature as an art. If an instructor could be satisfied with fitting boys and girls for examinations, nothing could be simpler or easier; but I am sure that I am right in believing that our public-school teachers are eagerly anxious to make of this study all that is possible in the line of developing and ennobling their pupils.

Every earnest teacher knows that literature cannot be taught by arbitrary methods. The handling of classes studying the masterpieces of genius must be shaped by the knowledge and the inspiration of the individual teacher or it is naught. Neither I nor another may give a receipt for strengthening the imagination, for instilling taste, for arousing enthusiasm. All that any book of this sort can effect, and all that I have endeavored to do, is to protest against methods that are formal and deadening, to offer suggestions which may—even if only by disagreement—help to make definite the teacher's individual ideas, and to warn against dangers which beset the path of all of us to whom is committed the high office of teaching this noble art.

The idea which I have hoped most strongly to enforce is the possibility of arousing in children, even in those bred without refining or intellectual influences, an appreciation of the spirit and the teachings of the great writers, a love for good books which may lead them to go on with the study after they have passed beyond the school-room. The best literature is so essentially human, it so truly and so irresistibly appeals to natural instincts and interests, that for its appreciation nothing is needed but that it be understood. To produce and to cultivate such understanding should be, I believe, the chief aim of any course in literature.

The understanding and the appreciation must of course vary according to the temperament and the responsiveness of the child. Miracles are not to be expected. No teacher need suppose that the street Arab and the newsboy will lie down with Browning and rise up with Chaucer; that Sally and Molly will give up chewing gum for Shakespeare, or that Tom, Dick, and Harry will prefer Wordsworth to football. In his own way and to his own degree, however, each child will enjoy whatever literature he has comprehended. As far as he can be made to care for anything not directly personal or appealing to the senses, he may be made to care for this. Nature has taken care of the matter of fitting children to understand and to love literature as it has prepared them to desire life. To bring the young into appreciation of the best that has been thought and recorded by man, there is but one way: make them familiar with it.

It is a mistake to suppose, moreover, that an especial sort of books is needed for children. A selection there should be, and it is manifestly necessary to exercise common sense in choice of works for study. A class that will be deeply interested in "Macbeth" would be simply puzzled and bored by "Troilus and Cressida." Childish games for the intellect there may be, as there are childish amusements for the body; but so far as serious training is concerned there is neither adult literature nor juvenile literature, but simply literature.

The range of the mind of a child is limited, and the experience demanded for the simplest comprehension of a work may be necessarily beyond the possible reach of child life.[15] The limitations of youth have, however, and should have, the same effect in literature as in life. They restrict the comprehension and the appreciation of the facts of existence, and equally they restrict the comprehension and the appreciation of the facts in what is read. The impressions which the child takes from what he sees or from what he reads are not those of his elders, although this is less generally true of emotions than of facts. The important point is that the impressions shall be vital and wholesome, and above all else that they be true with the actual verity of human experience. We all commit errors in the conclusions we draw from life; and children will make mistakes in the lessons they draw from books. Books which are wise and sane, however, will sooner or later correct any misconceptions they beget, just as life in time makes clear the false conclusions which life itself has produced.

I have spoken more or less about the enjoyment of this study by children, and it is difficult if not impossible to conceive that if a class is rightly handled most children will not find the work a pleasure. It is necessary, however, to be a little on our guard in the practical application of the principle that children get nothing out of literature unless they enjoy it. They certainly cannot enjoy it unless they get

-----

15  See pages 68-70.

something out of it; but it will hardly do to make the enjoyment of a class too entirely the test by which to decide what work the class shall do. Pupils should be stimulated to solid effort in the way of application and concentration, and I have already pointed out that in mastering the difficulties of literary language they should be made to do whatever drudgery is needed, whether they are inclined to it or not. They cannot, moreover, read with intelligence anything with real thought in it, until they have learned concentration of mind. Children, like their elders, value most what has cost something to attain, and facile enjoyment may mean after-indifference.

The contagion of enthusiasm is one of the means by which children are most surely induced to put forth their best efforts to understand and to assimilate. If the teacher is genuinely enthusiastic in his love for a masterpiece, even if this be something that might seem to be over the heads of the children, he arouses them in a way impossible of attainment by any other means. A boy once said to me with that shrewdness which is characteristic of youth, "My teacher didn't like that book, and we all knew it by the way she praised it." Sham enthusiasm does not deceive children; but they are always impressed by the genuine, and no influence is more powerful.

The most serious obstacle which teachers of literature to-day meet with, I am inclined to think, is the difficulty children have in seizing abstract ideas.[16] So long as study and instruction are confined to the concrete and the particular the pupil works with good will and intelligence. The moment the boundary is crossed into the region of the general, he becomes confused, baffled, and unable to follow. The algebra of life is too much for the brain which is accustomed to deal only with definite values. What is evidently needed all along the line is the cultivation of the reasoning powers in the ability to deal with abstract thought. Personally I believe that this could be best secured by the simplification of the work in the lower grades, and

---

16  See page 112.

by the introduction of thorough courses in English grammar and the old-fashioned mental arithmetic. If some forty per cent. of the present curriculum could be suppressed altogether, and then ten per cent. of the time gained given to these two admirable branches, the results of training in the lower grades, I am convinced, would show an enormous improvement. I may be wrong in this, and in any case we must deal with things as they exist; and the teacher of literature must accept the fact that he has largely to train his class in breadth of thinking. He will be able to deal with generalizations only so far as he is assured that his students will grasp them, and this will generally mean so far as he is able to teach them to deal with this class of ideas.

This book has stretched beyond the limits which in the beginning were set for it, and in the end the one thing of which I am most conscious is of having accomplished the emphasizing of the difficulties of the branch of work with which it is concerned. If I have done nothing more than that, I have discouraged where I meant to help; and I can only hope that at least between the lines if not in the actual statements may be found by the earnest and hard-working teachers of the land—that class too little appreciated and worthy so much honor—hints which will make easier and more effective their dealing with this most important and most difficult requirement of the modern curriculum.